Widow For A Season

Finding Your Identity in Christ

Kristine Pappas

Widow for a Season
Finding Your Identity in Christ

Unless otherwise noted, Scripture quotations are from the from the New American Standard Bible®, Copyright 1960, 1962, 1963, 1968, 1971, 1972, 1973, 1975, 1977, 1995 by The Lockman Foundation. Used by permission. (**www.Lockman.org**)

Scripture quotations marked KJV are from the Holy Bible, King James Version, 1611.

ISBN 10: 0-88469-308-2
ISBN 13: 978-0-88469-308-6
Christian Living/Practical Life/Women

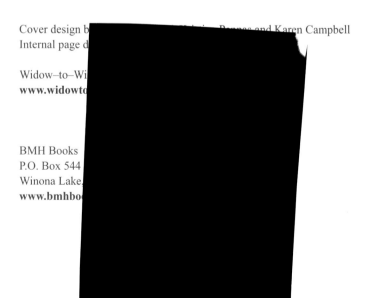

Cover design b⬛⬛⬛⬛⬛⬛⬛⬛⬛ ⬛⬛⬛⬛ ⬛⬛⬛⬛⬛ and Karen Campbell
Internal page d⬛⬛⬛⬛⬛

Widow–to–Wi⬛⬛⬛
www.widowt⬛

BMH Books
P.O. Box 544
Winona Lake⬛
www.bmhbo⬛

Dedication

For the "widows in their distress."

For the church that seeks to practice "pure and undefiled religion in the sight of our God and Father" (James 1:27).

For the friends and family who desire to come alongside as a source of encouragement and support.

May the Lord bless this tool in your hands for His glory.

Table of Contents

Preface

Wouldn't it be nice if life came with a manual?

As Christians we often ask this question even though we know that it does. The manual I refer to, of course, is the Bible. Sadly, however, we don't spend the necessary time in God's Word for it to help us when serious issues arise. Perhaps in your widowhood you can relate.

When my husband died of pancreatic cancer in 1998, leaving me with two teenagers at home, I was desperate. As I sought refuge in the Scriptures, I stumbled on the biblical promise that God is the husband to the widow (Isaiah 54:4) and father to the fatherless (Psalm 68:5), but I didn't know what that meant. I needed a resource that would translate God's Word into steps of practical application, because God's Word is our only hope. If we don't know how to make it work in our daily lives, we can't move forward.

Solomon wisely wrote, "But beyond this, my son, be warned: the writing of many books is endless, and excessive devotion to books is wearying to the body" (Ecclesiastes 12:12). Why have I written another book to add to the endless pile? Because this book uses God's Word as its template, not the wisdom of man. It is the compass that will drive you back to true north in the Word of God. And, like a beacon, the Word of God will draw you to Christ and His precious promises. This is a book that fleshes out the process of making truth work for you in your daily life.

But let us not be guilty like those written about in Hebrews. "The word they heard did not profit them, because it was not united by faith..." (Hebrews 4:2). The issue is how we trust God—where the rubber meets the road, so to speak. Does it really work? I have written this book to tell you, yes, it does work, but we must learn how to tap into its power. I pray that the message of this book will bless you and be a tool toward your complete healing.

But know that you will never be the same—that is God's plan.

Kristine Pappas
Columbus, Ohio
September 2006

Study Guide Format

Following each chapter you will find a set of questions that are designed to help you break down the information you have read. They are intended to help you identify and meditate on the principles presented in each chapter and personalize them. As you do so, you will move toward healing and develop practical applications toward life change. I hope you will also use this guide as a tool to draw other widows together and network with them for discussion and support.

A more extensive study is available at **www.widowtowidow.net** as well as other resources for encouragement. This site also contains an ongoing newsletter and an interactive segment where widows can encourage one another.

At the end of each chapter you will be asked to put specific Bible verses onto a key ring to be used for daily review and encouragement. To create this key ring you will need a 1¼" metal ring that you can open and close. The verses can be written on 3x5 index cards with a hole punched in the upper left–hand corner so they can be added to the ring.

General format to be used with each chapter:

After you read through each chapter, work on the following five key elements for personal application:

1. What biblical truths have you identified as precious promises from Christ for you to believe and act on that relate to each specific chapter theme?

2. What are the key verses that have had a special impact for you? These are the verses you will add to your key ring for your personal encouragement and review.

3. As you review the main themes of this chapter, write down what you think God's perspective is. Remember we are trying to think about things from the God–centered perspective of the thriver, not the self–centered orientation that operates from a victim/survivor mode.

4. What have you identified specifically in the context of this chapter that you personally need to think differently about? Write down the specific steps you will take to change what you think and how you act.

5. Now that you have worked through the above four steps, outline what godly goals you will set for yourself. Remember, these will be goals over which only you and God have control.

Finally, many additional study sheets can be accessed by logging on to our website at **www.widowtowidow.net** and choosing the Study Guide Tab. Each study is listed by chapter number and can be printed for personal or group use.

Part One:

Season Of Singleness

Chapter 1

Who Am I Now?

Defining Who We Are

❦

Have you ever attended a women's gathering in a roomful of unfamiliar faces? Usually the first order of business is for everyone to share something about who she is. Of course, we begin with our name and then typically share something about our personal circumstances like whether we are single, married, widowed, or divorced. Some may have jobs; others are stay-at-home moms. We may continue by telling about our role as wife, mother, grandmother, and so forth. No matter where we find ourselves in life, we usually have very definite perceptions about who we are. Those perceptions are the basis upon which we relate to others as well as to ourselves.

There are three critical factors that define who we are. The first factor concerns how we perceive ourselves in relation to our circumstances and the roles we play in them. This is our self-perception. The second factor concerns how we think others perceive us. How we manage *these* perceptions will determine whether or not we have healthy relationships with others. The third and most critical factor defining who we are concerns our relationship with Christ. I will refer to it throughout this book as our "identity in Christ."

Bringing Balance to Our Perceptions

There are some events in life that we will probably never fully comprehend. But we can accept even the most tragic events in life if we learn to interpret them through the lens of a healthy self-perception, healthy relationships with others, and a solid identity in Christ. Without this lens in place, we cannot understand suffering, tragedy, and death. Further, we cannot fully understand any event in life until we view it in the light of God's vast, eternal plan. We must find our center in God and work out from it instead of from the self-center of human psychology. God's ways are not our ways (Isaiah 55:8). Our life journey is not by our design but rather by His. We cannot use human means to explain God, but we can use His Word to understand ourselves and to make sense of our experiences. Without a connection to this God-center, we can never discover the true meaning of experiencing loss.

Bringing Balance to Our Roles

Even with healthy closure, our loss will always be a part of who we are. We must learn to live with that loss, but at the same time, we must not permit it to define us. In fact, we will not be able to operate from a God-center if we allow any experience or role to define us. For example, we can be mothers, but if motherhood is the total essence of who we are and if that role consumes us, who will we be when our children eventually step out from under that canopy? At the same time, we can be a wife. But if being a wife is what defines us, who will be left if our husband dies before we do?

That may be the question you are struggling with: *Who am I now that my husband is gone?* Losing a role we have become accustomed to can be a tremendous source of grief.[1] The role itself is often tied to our sense of worth and significance. How we perceive ourselves outside the roles of wife and mother will comprise a huge part of our redefinition as women. What is most important to a healthy recovery is to allow Christ to be the primary source of our definition. We must give Him permission to assign identity and value to our life. Everything must be evaluated against our identity in Christ. That is what it means to be God-centered and not self-centered in our outlook.

If we don't understand what it means to have a solid identity in Christ, we cannot see how this identity can help us work through difficult issues. First, however, we should consider the expected and predictable patterns we may already be exhibiting as a result of our loss.

Stages of Recovery

A person experiencing a life crisis such as losing a spouse will typically work through a continuum of three stages toward recovery: victim, survivor, and thriver.

These stages are a gauge of emotional and spiritual health. It is important to note that, although the goal is to develop the mindset of the thriver, accomplishing that goal does not mean you are finished with the mourning process. The term "thriver" merely identifies the emotional and spiritual health you want to achieve as you work through the mourning process.

These three stages may be unfamiliar to you. You are probably more familiar with the five stages of grief typically identified as denial and shock, anger, bargaining, depression, and acceptance. Elizabeth Kubler-Ross initially identified this five-stage process in an effort to explain the grief experience prior to death.[2] Although you may experience some of those same emotions as you grieve, the recovery stages we are discussing here are different. It was not until I attended a crisis and trauma intervention workshop conducted by Gregory Schad, a social worker with extensive experience in counseling trauma victims, that I began to rediscover the *me* I felt I had lost. Schad's understanding and expertise concerning the grief process resulting from trauma and crisis is invaluable to our discussion.

In the initial stages of our loss, we will encounter shock and/or denial no matter what the cause. Loss is loss, and the result will drive our pain, thoughts, and emotions. As we work through this initial shock and denial phase, we feel we are victims of circumstances beyond our control. We think of ourselves as victims without power or choice. We literally give the event permission to control us, and we may feel totally at its mercy.

As you work through this stage, you will experience anger and depression on many levels. Give yourself time and permission to grieve. You may experience withdrawal and apathy, restless agitation, tears, outbursts, and difficulty focusing or retaining information. If you are drawn to drinking or drug abuse, you should get special help and counseling.

This chart is taken with permission from the workshop entitled, "Care When It's Critical: Helping Others Recover from Trauma."[3]

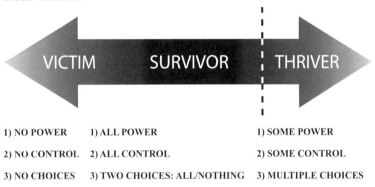

VICTIM	SURVIVOR	THRIVER
1) NO POWER	1) ALL POWER	1) SOME POWER
2) NO CONTROL	2) ALL CONTROL	2) SOME CONTROL
3) NO CHOICES	3) TWO CHOICES: ALL/NOTHING	3) MULTIPLE CHOICES

The longer we remain in this first stage, perceived victimization, the harder it will be to move on to the next stage of recovery, survival. In the survivor phase we may begin to pick ourselves up a bit and determine not to be a victim. Instead, we begin to take full control and power. We will interpret every choice as black and white—an "all or nothing" proposition. This need to control is driven from the pain we have experienced and the hopelessness that we feel. We will tend to grab control wherever we can. For some of us, this is when we take the reins from God. This attitude is a direct result of the conscious decision we have made about how to respond.[4] As long as we continue to allow our pain or our role as survivor to define us, we cannot move into the last phase, thriving. We can remain hopelessly stuck in either of the first two stages indefinitely.

If you have never acquired a stabilized, Christ-centered perspective of life, it will be very difficult to move into the final stage of recovery as a thriver. It is in this stage that you realize you have some power, some control, and multiple choices. Your choices become percentages of shades of gray. You begin to examine the pros and cons as you make decisions. The pain of being a victim is now under your control. In other words, the pain or trauma you have experienced is now just a season or a chapter in your life.[5]

My brother-in-law has a saying on his desk that captures this mind-set: "You cannot control the wind, but you can adjust the sails." The control you possess is in your response, not in the event. You will need to trust Christ and give your surrendered control to Him.

Recovery may not be automatic, but movement into the last phase of the continuum should begin within months, not years. The goal is to work through your grief and recovery from the perspective of the thriver rather than the victim or the survivor. The time frame for this movement will be greatly affected by your personal belief system.[6] Because you may get stuck in one or more of the phases in the process, it is important to evaluate where you are on the continuum.

Stage-stuck

It is unhealthy to settle in either of the first two stages for an extended period, because while you are in either of those stages, your emotional and spiritual perceptions will be dramatically impacted by their characteristics. Neither stage is Christ-centered.

As you attempt to protect yourself against further pain, unhealthy defense mechanisms may develop. Here is an example: After a negative event occurs in your life, you respond, *Well, it has to get better; it always does.* On the surface this line of thinking might appear to be positive evidence of placing your trust in Christ. Later, however, instead of moving on with a sense of peace, you might find yourself thinking, *It's just a matter of time before something bad will happen, so I won't get my hopes up.*[7]

As this unhealthy line of thinking develops into a habitual pattern, you will become fixed at this spot and your trust in the Lord will be seriously disabled. On and on you go around this loop of emotional protection, feeling that you have no power, no control, and no choices. Surprisingly, you perceive this as a place of safety. You may not want to leave it because, even though it is not a healthy or a happy place to live, it has become your comfort zone. It is safer than change, and it keeps you from experiencing a trust that you fear will end in disappointment.

We may also find ourselves lost in the survivor stage. We have taken control, though control from a human effort is hopeless outside of trust in Christ, and we are unable or unwilling to let go. Maybe we unconsciously remain there out of loyalty to those we have lost. We may feel that moving on leaves them behind forever. We can never move toward recovery, however, as long as we are stuck. God should always be the one who defines our self-perception. Here is where our faith can help us move toward the Christ-centered perspective of the thriver.

When I talk with Christians about their identity in Christ, they often are unclear about what that means. Our identity centers on our relationship with Christ. Do you go through life with a self-focused attitude that requires you to invite God into your trials, or do you have the sense that you and Christ are already experiencing them as one? Every trial and event that brings you pain is already on His map, not because He is causing it but rather He is allowing it to prepare you for eternity. Every trial is part of the process of becoming one with Christ—of becoming more Christ-like.

If our identity is in Christ, our expectations and the roles we play here on earth will be aligned with our eventual entrance into heaven. They will be tools in the greater plan God is working out in our lives. If we play the role of wife within our identity in Christ, our definition will not change when our husbands are taken from us. Our mission will continue because that family role was not our primary source of identification. Certainly, we will miss our husbands and their involvement with us, but we will be able to move on with Christ. We will have a much more balanced relationship with those around us if their expectations and roles do not control us. We will also be challenged to re-examine the expectations we place on others and ourselves.

Balancing Our Responses to Others

Jesus provides a good example for us in John's Gospel. After witnessing the many signs and wonders Jesus performed during a Passover feast in Jerusalem, the crowds "defined" Him and literally believed in His name. John, in John 2:24–25, alludes to the idea that Jesus did not need their affirmation to be who He was. The Scripture says that Christ did not commit, or as *Strong's Exhaustive Concordance* defines it "put [Himself] in trust with" the world around Him.[8] It was enough to follow exclusively what He heard the Father say to Him. He reveals this in John 5:17, 30 when He says, "My Father is working until now, and I Myself am working…I can do nothing on My own initiative…I do not seek My own will, but the will of Him who sent Me." Christ did not need to convince men or win their allegiance to His mission. They would play their roles in God's plan as they permitted God's interaction with them personally. Christ didn't have to influence them or be responsible for their actions. He is not controlled by our free will to choose. In our response to others' perceptions of us, we have to commit to this same practice.

Just as Christ's identity in the Father was embodied in Christ's mission, so our identity must be embedded in the mission that God has assigned to us. In Philippians 3:12 Paul instructs us by his own example to take hold of that for which Christ has taken hold of us. God already has a purpose for our lives. We are to be His ambassadors. He gives the directions and we follow. We do not need the affirmation of others because their opinion is secondary to our primary purpose. To look at life through these glasses is to see trials, loss, and suffering from a God-centered perspective.

Sometimes we have trouble identifying God's specific purpose for us. In John 6:28–29 Jesus' disciples said they wanted to work the works of God, but they didn't know what they were. Jesus told them that the work of God is to believe in Christ. In John 4:34 Jesus had explained that His *food* was to do God's will and to accomplish His work. Our mission is the same. This mission is defined in John 4:35–38 as sowing and reaping in a field "white for harvest." Our business for God is to be His hands and feet in reaching the lost.

In addition to reaching the lost, God also desires to glorify Himself—or to reveal Himself. We join Him in this mission when we are driven to Him through trials and others see *His strength* in us. Our participation in bringing both the lost to Christ and glory to God is the essence of our identity in Christ and our mission. This God-centered perspective is the one through which we must view every experience.

Co-dependency

Now that we have considered the internal dynamics of our identity and relationship with Christ, we will consider how unhealthy relationships with others can negatively affect our recovery from loss. The unhealthy relationships I refer to are those containing elements of a co-dependent nature. A co-dependent relationship involves the manipulation of one's behavior in an effort to meet emotional worth or needs. Typically as one party manipulates, the other cooperates. This manipulation can be physical, verbal, emotional, or psychological.

Because the dynamics of co-dependent relationships can be very destructive, it is important to consult a counselor or attend a co-dependent support group for help in managing them in a safe and healthy way. One good resource on co-dependency is *Boundaries, When to Say YES, When to Say NO to Take Control of Your Life* by Henry Cloud and John Townsend.[9]

When co-dependency is involved, the struggle to redefine our lives and follow God's direction may be frustrated by well-meaning family and friends. They may not accept our resistance to their opinions and may try to assert authority over us. If we are healthy, we should be able to take control of our lives and easily say no when appropriate. If we cannot resist their tactics and break free, then we need to get help.

It is also possible that we may be the one trying to manipulate others to keep things the way they have always been. We may find ourselves demanding others to respond in ways that selfishly satisfy our needs, unwilling to release them from our expectations. We must allow others to say no to our wishes. Then we need to redirect those concerns to God. These dynamics can be very subtle and hard to identify, and even when identified, they can be hard to change. It is important to examine your relationships for co-dependent tendencies, and it is even more important to get the help you need if you think those dynamics exist.

Chapter 1

Boundaries

Co-dependent relationships are created when boundary violations are allowed to go unchecked. According to Cloud and Townsend, "Boundaries define us. They define *what is me* and *what is not me*. A boundary shows me where I end and someone else begins, leading to a sense of ownership" (p. 29).

"In addition to showing us what we are responsible for, boundaries help us to define what is *not* on our property and what we are *not* responsible for. We are not, for example, responsible for other people. Nowhere are we commanded to have 'other-control,' although we spend a lot of time and energy trying to get it!" (p. 30).

Boundaries keep good things in and bad things out. Once we recognize where the boundaries are, we can begin to protect our freedom by staying within them, and they can become the alarm system that helps us know when to withdraw in healthy ways (Cloud and Townsend, pp. 24–33). In order to evaluate boundary violations in our relationships, we must first know what our boundaries are.

According to Cloud and Townsend, there are seven kinds of boundaries or lines that define others and us. They are skin, words, truth, geographical distance, time, emotional distance, and other people (pp. 33–37). As you think about difficult relationships, use these seven boundaries as a guide.

- *Skin* involves your physical person. Violation of this boundary might involve physical or sexual abuse.

- *Words* involve the freedom you feel to say no to the things that you do not want to participate in or to verbally express your feelings.
- *Truth* has to do with God's truth and the truth about you. Truth keeps you aligned with reality, which has everything to do with your identity in Christ.
- *Geographical distance* deals with the freedom you have to withdraw physically from danger, evil, or relationships in which you feel unsafe.
- *Time.* "Taking time off from a person, or a project, can be a way of regaining ownership over some out-of-control aspect of your life where boundaries need to be set" (Cloud and Townsend, p. 36). We must leave the use of and decisions about our time in God's control and not in the control of others who may demand it.
- *Emotional distance* is the only boundary that is considered temporary. It is a time-out period in relationships for the purpose of getting help with unacceptable and harmful behavior. This help may come from counselors and/or support groups.
- *Other people.* "There are two reasons why you need others to help with boundaries. The first is that your most basic need in life is for relationship…The other reason we need others is because we need new input and teaching… creating boundaries always involves a support network" (Cloud and Townsend, p. 37).[10]

As you move toward new identity in Christ as a thriver, co-dependent relationships will be threatened. You will no longer be available to act your part in the co-dependent relationship because Christ is now the focus of your life. This change can result in hurt feelings as relational dynamics shift.

When boundary violations result, the violators may attempt to punish you by withdrawing attention or approval until your behavior meets their expectations. Resistance to your change can take many forms of abuse: physical, verbal, emotional, and/or psychological. You must trust Christ for the courage to make the changes necessary for healthier bonds with others. As Paul said concerning the things Christ called Him to, "…forgetting what lies behind, and reaching forward to what lies ahead, I press on toward the goal for the prize of the upward call of God in Christ Jesus" (Phil. 3:13–14). You may have to let go of the familiar past to progress in your relationships. It is our unhealthy behaviors that we are leaving behind and a stronger identity in Christ that thrusts us forward.

You may find that sharing less with others and more with the Lord is better. If you feel like you have to present a marketing plan to gain someone's emotional permission for the plan God has given you, then you should re-evaluate the dynamics of that relationship. This does not mean you should quit the relationship but rather work to make it healthy. God won't let you down. Remember that God may not give anyone else the direction and information He gives you concerning your part in His will. Though He has brought you to a place where it seems no one else has been, *He* stands there with you.

As you examine this process of recovery, you will probably be able to identify your place on the journey from victim to thriver. I hope you are moving steadily forward and not getting stuck or mixing the order of progression. Be patient with yourself as you allow time for healing. Stay in God's Word for strength and direction. Don't let anyone or anything define you other than your identity in Christ and His mission for you. You are the only one who can determine the timetable of your recovery, and you must do everything necessary to work out that recovery as a thriver.

As you continue to work through this book, you may find that you are not ready to tackle some chapters—that's okay. The initial chapters lay the foundation for the rest. Read what meets your need now. You can always come back to the parts you skip. Don't try to do anything in your own strength; instead, lean only on Him.

Study Guide
Chapter 1: Who Am I Now?
(See page vi for instructions for using the study guide.)

1. Review the continuum stages of victim, survivor, and thriver. Which stage best describes where you are? If you do not see yourself as a thriver, ask God to help you make the necessary adjustments in your thinking. Make a list of the victim and survivor thought patterns you are practicing and outline the kind of thoughts you will start thinking in their place.

2. What are the key verses you have either read in this chapter or God has brought to mind that have had special impact for you? These are the verses you will need to add to your key ring for your personal encouragement and daily review.

3. Think about the roles that you played before the death of your husband. Some, like the role of wife, are no longer functional. Some roles may still be functioning but they have become frustrating and difficult to perform without your husband's involvement. How will you align these roles with the God-centered perspective we have examined? What different expectations will you set for these roles?

4. Take some time to think about the difficult relationships you may be struggling with because of the co-dependent elements you have learned about in this chapter. Write out the ways you will begin to respond differently. Ask God to give you strength for these changes. If these relationships seem beyond your ability to change, you should seek help from a co-dependent support group or a counselor. The degree to which others are able to control you will directly determine your emotional and spiritual health as you grieve and follow God's direction for recovery.

The steps outlined here mark the beginning of taking your thoughts captive and aligning them with the God-centered perspective that marks us as healthy thrivers.

For a deeper study about your identity in Christ and the roles He desires you to play in His kingdom work, go to **www.widowtowidow.net** and select Study Guide. You will see a tab for Chapter One and that will direct you to this material. Topics there for your consideration include:

- Examination of the role we play as ambassadors for Christ and the ministry of reconciliation
- An extensive listing of verses describing our identity in Christ
- Material on how to determine your spiritual gifts as well as a tool designed to help you determine your spiritual passion
- Materials that will help you deal with some of the difficult relationships you may have involving co-dependent issues such as guilt, forgiveness, and reconciliation

These studies include work sheets that can be printed from the site to review at your leisure.

Chapter 2

Bad News—Good News

Establishing Our Identity in Christ

❧

*I*magine going to the store to buy a lamp for your home or office. You bring the lamp home and cannot wait to see how nicely it complements your decor. You put in a new light bulb, eagerly plug in the lamp, and expect to see a bright light. To your dismay, though, the light is not forthcoming. You check the bulb to be sure it is not defective and it seems to be okay. Finally, you conclude that there is no power in the socket. Even though the lamp and bulb are in place and plugged into the power source, nothing is going to happen until power comes through that socket.

The Source of Truth: God's Word

Think about this book as that lamp. It contains the truth that can lead you to safety, courage, and victory in Christ. Without surrendering and receiving Him as Lord and Savior of your life, however, this truth will have no power for you. It will just be a book of worthless knowledge.

A young family friend recently went through a great personal trial with paralyzing anxiety. She had become totally imprisoned by her fear and emotions. She was unable to leave her house or get into her car and was on the verge of losing her job as well as her sanity. Yet she had grown up hearing about God and knowing a lot about the Bible. She prayed every day and tried with great effort to gain control of her life. She read God's Word but it was only a temporary help. She claimed that she believed in God and loved Him, but she was unable to find victory. Until she learned how to receive Jesus Christ by surrendering her will to His authority, she could not find peace.

Many others struggle with the same frustration of a faith that seems to be dead in the water. I pray that this chapter will help you discover Christ's power and find victory for the rest of your journey. Paul said in Romans 1:16, "For I am not ashamed of the gospel, for it is the power of God for salvation to every one who believes, to the Jew first, and also to the Greek."

Maybe you thought you had received Christ at some point in your past but are now unsure. Maybe, like my friend, you are doing everything your faith has taught but you are constantly defeated in your effort to overcome your trials. Perhaps, for the first time in your life, you are ready to surrender your life to Christ but you don't know how. The Lord tells us, "In a favorable time I have answered you, And in a day of salvation I have helped you" (Isaiah 49:8).

"Behold, now is 'the acceptable time,' behold, now is 'the day of salvation'" (2 Cor. 6:2).

The Source of Salvation: Christ's Sacrifice

God has accomplished our salvation with the peace and power that accompanies it through Jesus' sacrifice on the cross. Many people are uncertain about their role in the salvation process. They mistakenly assume that salvation is just believing that God exists. When asked about their assurance of going to heaven when they die, few will say with certainty they are eternally secure. God, however, does not provide weak and uncertain power that will not help us through trials and testings. Even the New Testament Jews thought they had met the conditions for salvation, but Paul revealed their true condition.

> For I testify about them that they have a zeal for God, but not in accordance with knowledge. For not knowing about God's righteousness and seeking to establish their own, they did not subject themselves to the righteousness of God. For Christ is the end of the law for righteousness to every one who believes (Romans 10:2–4).

The Means of Salvation: It's Your Choice

Jesus Christ will never force His salvation on anyone. He provided for it, but He requires us to choose whether or not we want it. That decision must be based not on what you think but on an understanding of the scriptural conditions Christ has established. We all make that decision at some point before we die.

We choose salvation because we want to spend eternity with the lover of our soul, Jesus Christ. If we do not choose to receive Christ, we will spend eternity in hell with Satan and his host of fallen angels, totally separated from God (Matt. 25:41). The torment of hell is not just hot fire or the suffering of its inhabitants. Hell is being totally separated from God and Christ forever with no chance to change that horrifying reality. Even if we have rejected Christ, we are still surrounded by His love because we continue to experience the presence of Christ through His creation and through Christians in our lives.

If we have not chosen to spend time with Christ here on earth, why would we want to spend eternity with Him? At the end of time, though, every knee will bow and every heart will have an unquenchable thirst and desire never to be separated from Him again (see Romans 13:11, 12). Then it will be too late to make changes. That will be the regret and agony of hell, and it will hurt so badly that it will be like a fire consuming us. This is vividly displayed in the story of Lazarus and the rich man found in Luke 16:19–31.

The choice to receive Christ and secure our place as His children is a scriptural idea. We read in John 1:12, "But as many as received Him, to them He gave the right to become children of God, even to those who believe in His name." This decision is often referred to in the Scriptures as "being born" or "born again." In John 3:5–7 Jesus explains to Nicodemus,

"Unless one is born of water and the Spirit he cannot enter into the kingdom of God. That which is born of the flesh is flesh, and that which is born of the Spirit is spirit. Do not be amazed that I said to you, 'You must be born again.'"

Without making this decision to receive Christ and what He offers, we are eternally lost. Think of it in terms of a political election. You may have researched the candidates carefully, and you may be knowledgeable about the best choice for the office. But if you don't cast your vote, your choice will never be counted. It will be as though you made no choice at all. Similarly, if you fail to accept Christ, it's the same as willfully rejecting Him.

The Need for Salvation: Sin

The first step in deciding whether or not you want to choose Christ is to consider why Jesus went to the cross in the first place. It is widely understood that He died to take away our sins. That means, though, that if we are not willing to admit we are sinners, the cross cannot apply to us. Christ cannot be separated from the cross. God says, "For all have sinned and fall short of the glory of God" (Rom. 3:23). That is bad news for us. The good news, however, is in Romans 5:8, "But God demonstrates His own love toward us, in that while we were yet sinners, Christ died for us."

When we acknowledge that we are sinners, we must recognize that we are without hope. "For the wages of sin is death" (Romans 6:23). "Behold, the Lord's hand is not so short That it cannot save; Nor is His ear so dull That it cannot hear. But your iniquities have made a separation between you and your God, And your sins have hidden His face from you so that He does not hear." (Isaiah 59:1–2). These same sins were the reason God forsook Christ, His own Son, as evidenced in the ninth hour on the cross when Jesus cried out, "My God, my God, why have You forsaken Me?" (Matthew 27:46).

And what is sin exactly? Paul says in Romans 14:23, "…whatever is not from faith is sin." Whatever you are not trusting Christ for in your life will result in sin. We must not place our trust in any authority other than Christ. He must always remain on the throne of our lives. James tells us that "…each one is tempted when he is carried away and enticed by his own lust. Then when lust has conceived, it gives birth to sin: and when sin is accomplished, it brings forth death" (James 1:14–15). God reveals to us as early as Genesis that "The intent of man's heart is evil from his youth" (Genesis 8:21).

Jesus told us in Revelation 3:19 to be zealous to repent because He rebukes those He loves. That is a very important element in receiving Christ. When we come to terms with our sin, we usually want to make that sin right before God—we want Him to know we are sorry. Repentance, though, is more than just saying you are sorry for your sin. *Strong's Exhaustive Concordance* defines repentance as a reversal of your decision.[1] It means to turn and go in the opposite direction. This reversal is the demonstration of repentance, and it is an outward reflection of what is really in one's heart.

The Locus of Salvation: the Heart

The heart is what God sees and where He does His mighty works in us. What is in our heart is important because it determines how we conduct ourselves in life—how we make decisions. Hannah Whitall Smith writes,

> I am convinced that throughout the Bible the expressions concerning the "heart" do not mean the emotions, that which we now understand by the word "heart," but they mean the will, the personality of the man, the man's own central self; and that the object of God's dealing with man is that this "I" may be yielded up to Him, and this central life abandoned to His entire control.[2]

What is in our heart will rule our decisions and conversations. Jesus said, "For the mouth speaks out of that which fills the heart" (Matthew 12:34). And what should our mouths be speaking?

In Romans 10: 9–10, Paul writes, "That if you confess with your mouth Jesus as Lord, and believe in your heart that God raised him from the dead, you will be saved; for with the heart a person believes, resulting in righteousness, and with the mouth he confesses, resulting in salvation." We must believe that Jesus was the Son of God raised from the dead but realize that "…the devils also believe [that there is one God], and shudder" (James 2:19). This belief alone is not saving faith. You must confess with your mouth Jesus as Lord. This is a faith that surrenders the will and choice totally to Christ. He becomes our Lord as though we were His slaves. It is a faith that believes in God but also believes what God says and responds in obedience to His will and promises.

The Evidence of Salvation: Obedience

God asks us to place ourselves under His authority. Jesus Christ had this attitude in His relationship with the Father and He desires the same of us. He said in John 5:30, "I can do nothing on My own initiative. As I hear, I judge; and My judgment is just, because I do not seek My own will, but the will of Him who sent Me." Jesus Christ was totally surrendered to His Father. That surrender was evidence of a spiritual oneness with the Father, a oneness so important to Him that He prayed God would bring us into that same relationship. He was praying for His apostles when He said, "I do not ask on behalf of these alone, but for those also who believe in me through their word [that is, believers today]; that they may all be one; even as You, Father, are in Me, and I in You, that they also may be in Us, so that the world may believe that You sent Me" (John 17:20, 21). Our decision to surrender to Christ brings salvation to us and gives evidence of Him to a lost world that is watching. It is an intimate, personal relationship with a holy God. How powerful!

Here's the bottom line: "How shall we escape if we neglect so great a salvation? After it was at the first spoken through the Lord, it was confirmed to us by those who heard" (Hebrews 2:3). If you acknowledge that you are a sinner without hope and repent of your sin, confessing with your mouth Jesus *as* Lord, and believing that God raised Him from the dead, praise God, you are saved! (Rom. 10:10). God has heard you. Life will be forever different.

The Results of Salvation: Benefits

Here are a few of the wonderful benefits of the decision to surrender to Christ. These are some of the promises of God that He will faithfully perform as you continue in your relationship with Him.

- You are a new creature (2 Corinthians 5:17).
- You are renewed in the spirit of your mind (Ephesians 4:23).
- Your name is written in the Book of Life (Revelation 3:5, 20:15).
- You have been spiritually baptized into Christ, clothing yourself with Him (Galatians 3:27).
- You are one Spirit with the Lord (1 Corinthians 6:17).
- You are spiritually seated with Him in heaven at the right hand of God (Ephesians 2:6). This is important because it is a place of authority. Christ could not sit there until God put all authority under His feet (1 Cor. 15:24–25, 27). As we are seated with Him, we have that same authority through Him to stand against spiritual attack. (See chapter 5 on spiritual warfare.)
- You are sealed with the Holy Spirit of promise which is your guarantee of the eternal life you will inherit (Ephesians 1:13, 14).

- You have been bought with a price and are now the spiritual dwelling place of the Holy Spirit (1 Corinthians 6:20, 21).
- The Holy Spirit teaches you the things of God and searches your heart (1 Corinthians 2:10–13).
- The Holy Spirit convicts you of sin (John 16:8).
- The Holy Spirit interprets your prayers (Romans 8:26).
- God begins to woo you into an interactive relationship with Him where He speaks to your mind and you respond to Him in meditation and prayer. He says that if we seek Him we will find Him if we seek Him with all of our heart (Jeremiah 29:11–13).
- You have assurance of eternal life through Christ and no power can change that (1 John 5:13, John 10:25–30).
- You are the righteousness of God (2 Corinthians 5:21).
- You are an ambassador for Christ (2 Corinthians 5:20).

Finally, "If you have been raised up with Christ, keep seeking the things above, where Christ is, seated at the right hand of God. Set your mind on the things above, not on the things that are on earth. For you have died and your life is hidden with Christ in God. When Christ, who is our life, is revealed, then you also will be revealed with him in glory" (Colossians 3:1–4).

Study Guide

Chapter 2: Bad News—Good News
(See page vi for instructions for using the study guide.)

1. If after reading this chapter, you realize you have never consciously surrendered your life to Christ in a personal decision that has resulted in a life change, please take this moment to review the following New Testament verses and follow their direction. Ask God to direct your thoughts and understanding as you read.

> 2 Corinthians 6:2
>
> Romans 3:23–24
>
> Romans 6:23
>
> 1 John 1:8–10
>
> 2 Corinthians 7:9–10
>
> Romans 10:9–10

There are many ways to take this step in a private moment of prayer. Pray from your heart. You are alone with God. Just confess to Him that you are a sinner, that you believe Jesus died for your sins and He is the resurrected Lord, and that you want Him to be Lord of your life. It's pretty simple and you can't get it wrong, because Jesus knows what is in your heart already and He is more interested in that than anything you say.

2. Now add these verses to your key ring:

    John 1:12–13

    Acts 8:26–39

    Titus 3:5–7

    Acts 2:41–42

    Romans 12:4–5

3. Be excited about this decision and share it with others. A confession of faith is usually followed by water baptism as in the case of Philip and the Ethiopian eunuch (Acts 8:26–39). So take that step as well. If you don't have a church family, now is the time to look around to find a place to become involved.

Additional studies can be accessed at **www. widowtowidow.net** in Chapter Two under the Study Guide Tab on subjects such as:

- Security in Salvation and the Process of Judgment
- Understanding our Role as Ambassadors for Christ.

Chapter 3

Lost To Be Found
The View From God's Word

❧

I remember as if it were yesterday—the joy I felt in anticipation of having my first child. I was excited and confident about my decision to breastfeed. I had done all the research on the topic and performed every nipple-toughening exercise in the La Leche League Manual, *The Womanly Art of Breastfeeding*. After all, I was a registered nurse! What else did I need to know? I had the knowledge all right, but the actual experience was something else indeed.

You haven't really experienced the *joy* of breastfeeding until you have realized the agony of engorged breasts whose "milk hasn't come in yet" or bleeding nipples that send you through the ceiling every time your little darling wants to nurse. It gives real meaning to the term "bite the bullet." As your baby grows, he needs to build up the milk supply, which means an increased nursing schedule, and you begin to dread the sweeping hand of the clock.

After trying everything I had learned to overcome the cracks and bleeding from each nursing session, I finally called the pediatrician. A wise and knowledgeable nurse sensed my suffering and pain. She also knew that the truth she was about to share would either disqualify me from this race or give me the ammunition to win. She very honestly said to me, "Honey, to be completely healed, this process is going to take another six weeks." I will never forget the jarring realization of what that meant for me. Through tear-filled eyes, I listened very carefully to her instructions. When I hung up the phone, I knew there would be no quick fix. If I were to succeed in accomplishing what was so very important to me, I had to make a decision. Did I want to overcome this or not? By deliberate choice, I decided I would do whatever was required until I either succeeded or died trying.

That illustration might sound dramatic to you, but if you are a recent widow you are daily facing some very tough decisions. Just like the truths the nurse shared with me, you will have to make some hard choices with the truths you embrace. I wonder sometimes why that nurse didn't just lie to me to soften the blow, but I realize now that it was truth that empowered me to set my course. You are where you are by God's permission, and even though He had the ability to prevent this from happening to you, He didn't.

When my husband died, I remember thinking, *"I am a strong woman of God. I will eventually get over this. Someday this will be my past and not my present."* But that just isn't so. Like everything else we encounter in life, our experiences will always remain with us to some degree because we are defined by them and our identity will rise out of them as the Potter works at the clay.

God is faithful. Jeremiah 29:11–14 in the King James Version has become the guiding Scripture for my life.

> For I know the thoughts that I think toward you, saith the Lord, thoughts of peace, and not of evil, to give you an expected end. Then shall ye call upon me, and ye shall go and pray unto me, and I will hearken unto you. And ye shall seek me, and find me, when ye shall search for me with all your heart. And I will be found of you, saith the Lord.

Trusting God's Promises

In the initial stages of my widowhood I began to realize that I was desperately ignorant of the promises of God. It's not that I didn't know my Bible, but what I now claim as the powerful promises of God that help me through the day were just not coming to mind. It's clear to me now that God was busy at work. He provided much for me, but I couldn't see it. His provision had been set in motion years before.

In my breastfeeding illustration I said that the truth had empowered me. That is true, but initially it just knocked me off my feet. The Lord began almost immediately to use certain people in my life. One of my good friends lost her husband about nine months after I lost mine and our lives tragically collided. Then the Lord brought me into a circle of several other widows who were a bit further along in their recovery. I was driven to know their journey and how long it would take for me to be whole again. I was looking for a magical and quick formula to recovery.

My friend and I sat down with one woman who had been widowed for ten years. I will never forget hearing her say that she finally began living after the eighth year. Another widow told us that in the four years she had been a widow the fourth was the worst. These were crushing blows to my belief that I could easily get back on track.

Since I have always been an overcomer, this reaction was contrary to my nature. I take what's wrong and make it right. I'm the one who makes lemonade out of the lemons in life. For the first time, though, I was beginning to think that maybe I couldn't pull it off this time. That is exactly what God wanted me to discover. I could never do it by myself. The faith that had always worked for me was crumbling for the sake of a greater, more perfect one.

Misunderstood Truths

As a result of my own experience and my talks with other widows, God has revealed some truths I now realize widows commonly misunderstand. One such truth that Satan uses effectively against us rises out of the way our faith is tied and intertwined with our husband's. We don't recognize where his ends and ours begins. Being yoked in a marital relationship creates a faith oneness, similar in some ways to the oneness we have in Christ. A certain confident faith develops out of that relationship. When we lose our husband, an important element of our faith confidence is also lost. It is not lost altogether, but we have to be aware of that loss as we, as single believers, begin to rediscover and redefine our faith.

The same process occurs in the development of our children's faith. As we share our faith with our children, it becomes a strong anchor for them. They gain security in knowing we believe and practice the same faith alongside them. They experience their faith as an extension of ours and that gives them confidence. At some point, though, they have to step out to see it work for themselves apart from us.

It is the same for widowed women. Whether your husband knew the Lord or was spiritually weaker than you makes no difference. You hesitate when that companion is taken. The enemy will use that hesitation to cripple and take advantage of you. He will try to shake your faith. He wants to rob your courage, your confidence in your own choices, and most of all your confidence in God. Bottom line—who are we really trusting?

I thought I had an unshakable faith, but it was to be greatly tested. And that was the best thing that could have happened to me. I developed a stronger faith deep within me and God taught me how to use it in a powerful way. Just as we use only a small percentage of our brain potential, so I fear we under use the power God has made available to us through faith.

My purpose in this book is to share what God has been teaching me so you or someone you know who is going through this experience can find hope in the journey as well. As I struggled with my husband's death, I found myself searching God's Word for healing from this gaping heart wound. The greatest encouragement came from my pastor and his constant reminders of God's great and precious promises. I had always considered myself to be a serious student of God's Word. But God was using this pastor to direct me to truths concerning widows that I had not been aware of before. They challenged me to begin a study of the widow from a biblical perspective. I wanted to know what God's heart for the widow really is.

If we are to gain understanding, we must have a heavenly perspective. God's Word is the only source from which to gain His perspective. "For the word of God is quick, and powerful, and sharper than any two-edged sword, piercing even to the dividing asunder of soul and spirit, and of the joints and marrow, and is a discerner of the thoughts and intents of the heart" (Hebrews 4:12). Both the Old and New Testaments have clear directives about God's provision for widows. Notice in the following Scripture passages how attentive God is to the needs of widows and how He promises to avenge their mistreatment. Note, also, the widow's place of privilege.

God's Promises for the Widow

His Provision for Her

- Genesis 38:11. In Jewish custom if a childless woman became a widow, her husband's brothers were to produce children with her. See Genesis 38:6–26 and Deuteronomy 25:5–10 for examples. How tender of God to provide for this woman so she could have the joy and satisfaction of raising children for her husband's namesake!

- Deuteronomy 10:18. God Himself executes judgment for the widow and shows His love by providing food and clothing. Believe this powerful promise from God!
- Deuteronomy 14:28, 29; 26:12, 13. Every three years the annual tithe was to be brought for the needs of the widow, Levite, stranger, and fatherless. Remember, God owns it all. His storehouse is full! And He is able to distribute His wealth. He lays on the hearts of His faithful ones a desire to minister to those in need. His people are merely containers for His wealth. Is there anything your Father cannot provide? Did you ask for what you need? Or when it was offered did your pride prevent you from receiving it?
- Deuteronomy 24:18–22. Israel was instructed not to harvest their crops clean but to leave the droppings for the widow. Read the book of Ruth for a beautiful picture of this gleaning provision. Have you ever noticed that God has the most creative ways of providing what we need? Don't look for God to provide only through the obvious. I have learned to be excited about what God will do for my needs. Whatever the issue, I now respond, "I don't know what God would do, but I know that He already has something in mind."
- 1 Kings 17. During a period of great famine in Israel, God used the widow at Zarephath to provide for His prophet Elijah. Although God told her ahead of time that He intended to use her, she didn't provide pleasant hospitality. Instead, she was bitter (v. 12). This widow lived in an idolatrous nation and did not look at her

life from God's perspective. When her son died, even though she had seen the power of God through Elijah, her knowledge was not united with faith. Instead of trusting God, she blamed Elijah and his God (vv. 17, 18). She is able to acknowledge the Lord as God (v. 24) only when He heals her son and meets her need. She responds to life from her limited perspective unaware she was being used in God's greater plan.

Are we guilty of trusting God through the plenty but forgetting Him in the famine? Somehow, in our twisted way of thinking, we feel God is out to get us. We wonder what we have done to deserve our lot in life as if the whole world revolves around us. Like the widow at Zarephath, we may not be aware of how God is using us. That is one reason many widows find themselves in a fog about what they should be doing. They have lost their purpose and meaning in life. The secret is to figure out what part you are to play in God's plan instead of what part He is to play in yours. Will you let God show Himself to you through your need, or will you shake your fist at Him? Have no doubt there is a bigger plan at work and it's all about God.

- Psalm 68:5. "A father of the fatherless and a judge for the widows, Is God in His holy habitation."
- Psalm 146:9. The Lord protects the stranger and supports the widow, another promise of God's provision and protection.
- Isaiah 1:17, 23. The nation of Israel was commanded to plead for the widow, and Israel's leaders were criticized because they did not consider her cause.

- Isaiah 54:4, 5. The LORD of hosts, the Holy One of Israel, the God of the whole earth is the widow's husband and Redeemer. This is a powerful promise from God. Accept it. What could defeat us with God as our defender and husband?
- Jeremiah 7:6, 7. Treatment of widows was a qualifying criterion for God's blessings. Many times in Scripture, godliness is evaluated by the treatment of widows (see James 1:27). The tragedy of September 11, 2001, challenges our nation to respond to the needs of widows and the fatherless from that event.

His Protection of Her

- Exodus 22:22–24. If anyone afflicts a widow and she cries out to God, He will kill the offender, leaving his wife as a widow and his children fatherless. We need not be concerned about those who might take advantage of our situation. God is watching over us, and He will respond appropriately. This promise should give peace to our hearts.
- Deuteronomy 24:17. A widow's garment could not be taken in pledge. In other words, her word is her bond. Be sure your character before your community assures that your word will never be in question.
- Deuteronomy 27:19. Anyone who perverted the judgment of the widow was cursed. Only after I became a widow did I think much about how I may have treated widows. I think I had been unaware of them, but I would certainly not want to be among the cursed.

- Psalm 94:4–6. It is the workers of iniquity who slay the widow. They are our enemies so we must pray for them (Psalm 109:1–4). Let God take vengeance, as it is His to exercise on our behalf (Rom. 12:19).
- Proverbs 15:25. God promises to establish the border of the widow. The ancient boundary the fathers had set was not to be removed (Proverbs 22:28). When the children of Israel entered the Promised Land, each man put boundary marks around his property, which his children would inherit. They were warned not to remove the marks "which the ancestors have set, in your inheritance" (Deut. 19:14). Trust God to keep your home secure for you. It is your boundary. Many widows are ultimately faced with the decision to sell their home because of financial difficulties. If you are going to sell your home, trust God for the details. He will establish and keep the new boundaries for you. If you are having difficulty selling, trust God for His protection. His plan will be better than you might think.
- Proverbs 23:10–11. God warns His people not to move the ancient boundary or to go into the fields of the fatherless because our Redeemer is strong and will plead the case against us. Again, when we are walking with and trusting God, He will protect us unconditionally.
- Jeremiah 22:3; Zech. 7:10. Do not mistreat or do violence to the widow.
- Malachi 3:5. God promises to be a swift witness against those who oppress the widow.

Other Scriptures

- Numbers 30:9–16. A woman is bound to any commitment she makes with which her husband agrees. If he disagrees, he will bear her guilt (v. 15) and the Lord will forgive her (v. 12). She is bound, however, to any vow she makes after her husband's death. It may be difficult to accept, but Scripture reveals that our feminine nature is more easily deceived. For that reason, we are intended by God to be under the leadership of our husbands. That should not be considered demeaning, but rather providing a place of protection. We need to trust the wisdom of the decisions we made while our husbands were living. They may include financial direction as well as plans for our children. There will be new issues to work through on our own, but those that have already been planned should not be a source of unrest for us. God has promised to stand in place of our husbands, who are no longer there.

- Mark 12:38–40. The scribes were accused of devouring widows' houses, possibly taking them in lieu of taxes. Today we should do our homework to protect ourselves from financial unfairness. Be sure to research well those whom you trust with financial decisions. Don't hesitate to change course if you are not in agreement with the decisions of your financial advisors. If they are intimidating you in any way, take it as the Spirit's leading to go elsewhere. Get a second opinion, if necessary.

- Luke 7:12–15. Jesus demonstrated His compassion for the widow when He raised from the dead the only son of the widow of Nain.
- Luke 21:1–4. Jesus commends the poor widow because, out of her poverty, she placed into the treasury "all that she had to live on." This showed her total trust in God's provision for her. If you have not been giving a portion of your income to the Lord, you should begin to do so. You might use the Old Testament standard of 10 percent or ask God to direct you in the amount to give. This should become a consistent practice. God will richly bless your faithful acknowledgement of Him as your provider, and you will never see your needs go unmet.
- Acts 9:36–41. Dorcas, who may have been a widow herself, met the needs not only of other widows but of the poor as well. She was a powerful testimony of godliness through her sewing. Many times we widows feel confused about our worth and mission in life without our husbands. In *All the Women of the Bible*, Herbert Lockyer writes,

> The question came to Dorcas as it did to Moses when he felt he was not the man to deliver Israel from Egyptian bondage, "What is that in thine hand?" And Moses answered, "A rod" (Exodus 4:2). And that rod became the symbol of delegated divine power. "What is that in thine hand?" the Lord asked Dorcas. She said, "A needle,"

and He took what she had and she stitched for Christ's sake. All praise, then, to the needle that represented practical benevolence among the needy. The garments Dorcas cut out and sewed represented Christian faith in action. "I was naked and ye clothed me," said Jesus of those who clothed His poor and destitute children.

Dorcas' death was so devastating in the community that Peter was called to raise her from the dead! What a challenge to our reputation as widows in our own communities! What is it that is in our hand? It doesn't have to be a needle as it was with Dorcas. Would our ministry and character in Christ be worthy of Peter's same consideration? Are we known as servants using whatever talent we have for God's kingdom and glory, or are we whining complainers defined by idleness and gossip?

The Church's Role Toward Widows

Timothy clearly defines the church's role toward widows. The church is to honor widows who are widows "indeed." According to the Greek words *"chera"* and *"chasma,"* as defined by *Strong's Exhaustive Concordance*, a widow is a woman lacking a husband. The definition suggests a vacancy or impassable interval, a gulf.[2] In other words, it is a permanent, irreversible condition. The word "indeed," comes from the Greek word *"ontos,"* and refers to truth with certainty.[3]

According to Jewish custom, the widow's children and nephews also had a responsibility for her provision (v. 4). Remember that the childless widow was to be given to her husband's brother to perform the husband's duty in giving children (see Deut. 25:5). Perhaps that is the reason the nephew is directed to be responsible for her care as her own child would have been if she had children.

Timothy describes two widows. One is godly, the other, godless. They are the desolate widow who "has fixed her hope on God, and continues in entreaties and prayers night and day," and "she who gives herself to wanton pleasure [and] is dead even while she lives" (vv. 5–6).

A widow's family (v. 4) was to care for her or be counted worse than an infidel. In today's society the inability to care for a family's widows may be because they live at a distance from them. In the early church most families were nearby so it was easier to meet daily needs. Today's church leadership must take this social shift into account when considering the needs of the widows in their church families (vv. 7–8).

To be taken into the physical care of the church, a widow had to meet certain conditions: she was to be more than sixty years old, the wife of one man (suggesting she had not remarried), well known for good works. She was to have brought up children, showed hospitality, washed the saints' feet, helped those in trouble, and devoted herself to good works. In other words, she was a faithful, godly woman. If at all possible, though, she was to be taken care of by her believing children if she had them (vv. 9–10, 16).

A younger widow (under sixty years old by the age criterion of verse 9) may not have the spiritual discipline to remain pure outside a marital relationship. This purity refers first to sexual desires, which the passage suggests can be dealt with only by a mature relationship with God (v. 5). Second, purity that results from a productive godly use of time is required (v. 10) in contrast to being busybodies and gossips (v. 13). For these reasons younger widows are directed to remarry, have children, and manage their homes (vv. 11–14).

These instructions for the church were given to a culture that cared for a widow's total needs. In that culture, women often did not own anything and could not sustain themselves. A widow needed the basic provisions to survive, or she would become a homeless beggar or an indentured servant. In today's society with welfare, Social Security, women in the workplace, and a non-socialist community, it is assumed that a woman would not have the same needs for the church to meet. Consequently, few churches have programs to care for widowed members on any significant level. Stanley Cornils, pastor emeritus of the First Baptist Church, Vallejo, California, writes about today's church and its responsibility to the widow.

> In the course of a single year, 500,000 American wives become widows. A large percentage of these are members of our churches. My experience as a pastor leads me to believe that they form one of the most neglected segments of our church life. Certainly we

have a spiritual obligation to them. But what is it? And how can we perform it? For years I was overwhelmed by guilt feelings because I knew I had not ministered to them adequately. The Grecian Jews within the early church complained, "because their widows were being overlooked" (Acts 6:1), and most widows in our churches could echo their discontent. The leaders of the church then appointed leaders to look after this responsibility. A lack of satisfactory service brought this body into existence. Clearly, in the early church this service was to take a high priority. How much do your deacons know about caring for the widows of the congregation? Let me suggest four steps we can take to minister to widows in our churches: First, deal with major causative factors behind widows' problems by educating your congregation to prepare for the eventuality of death.

A widow's first and most difficult problem is that of working through her grief. But second, and often more frustrating, is coping with the financial management of the family, home, a business, an estate and investments. At the moment her husband dies, she crash-lands into an unfamiliar world of difficult decisions just when emotionally she is least capable of dealing with them.

All too often a husband deludes himself into acting as though he will live forever. Sylvia Porter reports that only three out of ten men have an up-to-date will. He fails to share business, legal and financial interests with his wife. Then, in seven cases out of ten, he dies before she does, leaving behind inadequate life insurance, a mortgaged home and an estate that is a disorganized and undecipherable mess.

Couples of all ages should be encouraged to face up to these probabilities and start making the in-case-something-should-happen-to-us decisions. These statistics don't lie. In most areas, an attorney for less than $100 can write a simple will.

I believe a Christian husband is morally obligated, to the best of his ability, to insure the welfare of his wife and children after he has been removed from the scene. I think this is part of what Paul meant in 1 Timothy 5:8: "But if any one does not provide for...those of his household, he has denied the faith and is worse than an unbeliever."

Second, early in her experience of aloneness, encourage a widow to join a widows-helping-widows group. No one can help a widow as effectively as another widow. If you have even a handful of recently widowed women in your congregation, why not start such a group? It will only take a little guidance on what to do and how to go about it, plus a list of helpful books on widowhood (which should be in your church library). Then the members will be off and running on their own, helping each other and winning other widows to Christ and your church.

Third, follow the lead of the early church and designate a deacon or someone else to look after the needs of each widow. The apostle James had much to say about practical religion. In James 1:27 he emphasized that "pure religion in the sight of our God and Father [is] to visit the orphans and widows in their distress—and what distress widowhood is! We should not interpret this passage outside the context of the Holy Writ; this is not all there is to "pure religion," but this *is* a part, and it should be given high priority.

Thayer's Greek-English Lexicon gives the Hebraistic meaning of the word "*episkeptomai,*" translated "visit" as "to look upon in order to help or benefit, to look after, to have a care for, provide for." Just to make a social call will not fulfill James's injunction.

So if a deacon or layman is appointed to visit a widow in his charge at least once a month over a period of, say, two years, this is what it means: When he makes his call and finds the bathroom faucet dripping, he fixes it. If the lawn needs mowing and there are no able-bodied children in the family to do it, he mows it. If the roof leaks, he repairs it. If the house needs painting and she cannot afford to have it done, he will recruit others in the fellowship to do the job so she will be proud of her home. If she needs counsel in business and financial matters and he does not feel qualified in this area, he will recommend the right person.

Finally, provide each widow with the names, addresses, and telephone numbers of the persons and agencies in the community to whom she can go for help. The pastor or widow's deacon should list realtors, bankers, social workers, counselors, a mechanic who won't overcharge for auto repairs and so on. Ascertain what her needs are and then do all you can to see that they will be met."[4]

Regardless of the responsibility a church may take for its widows, we have many precious promises from God about His commitment to us. I have found Him to be the faithful husband He promised to be, and I have been amazed at how He moves His hand for the widow who will trust Him completely for her every need.

Study Guide
Chapter 3: Lost to Be Found

(See page vi for instructions for using the study guide.)

1. This chapter is full of precious promises for you to claim. Do you realize that God is serious about His relationship with you? Make a list of the special promises that have encouraged you personally. Begin to act on these promises and believe that God will fulfill them in your life. Know that God is faithful.

2. What are the key verses that have had a special impact for you? These are the verses you will add to your key ring for personal review and encouragement.

3. If you are a new Christ-follower and are not yet involved with a church family, you must make finding one your priority now. God often works through our church family to provide for our needs. You are vulnerable to the enemy when you are not under the protection of Christ through a church. This also applies to believers who have stopped fellowshiping with a church.

4. What have you identified specifically in the context of this chapter that you need to begin thinking differently about in terms of a God-centered perspective? Write out each one and begin to think about how to make that mental adjustment.

Additional studies can be accessed at **www. widowtowidow.net** in Chapter Three under the Study Guide Tab on subjects such as:

- A Season of Singleness
- Other Precious Promises from God.

Part Two:

Season Of Strength

❦

Chapter 4

A Twist On Trust

Application For Trusting God

❧

A Tested Trust

The one thing that has made all the difference in my struggle with the unexpected loss of my husband is something a godly man shared with me early in my husband's illness. His advice was simple—"Just trust in God." That is the only advice he would ever give me! It was like a broken record every time he counseled me. There were some tough times when I wanted to scream at him, *But that just isn't doing the job! It isn't enough!* I am thankful now that he just kept directing me back to the Lord. He had to know my faith was weak, but trusting God was the only source of lasting power.

I had never experienced anything that so tested my ability to trust God, as did the untimely death of my husband. I prayed and confessed that I trusted God, but there was no comfort or peace in my heart. Fear convinced me that I had lost my way. I was desperate for control but I was trying to control all the wrong things. There were days when I couldn't convince myself that my husband wasn't just gone temporarily—like on a business trip or on guard duty. He would be home soon. On other days I felt as if he were someone I had only imagined and he never really existed. I'm sure I went through many stages of grief. I prayed and cried a lot. Nothing seemed familiar in my upside-down world. I didn't know who I was anymore, and I didn't know what I was supposed to do with myself every day. I woke up every morning, but when I looked in the mirror, I didn't see anyone looking back. It was like I had vanished, but where did I go?

When people said, "Just trust in the Lord," I thought of it as a cliché—it was what Christians said to one another in hard times. I had quipped similar words to others myself, but felt insulted by them now. Tagging the admonition to "trust in the Lord" as *cliché*, however, waters down the importance of its message. Over and over in Scripture *God's* admonition to those facing impossible challenges was always "Trust in me." His own example suggests that these are the most powerful words we can utter.

What makes us angry about these words is the challenge they place on our faith. They expose a weak relationship with Christ when we are unable to find strength in them. But when the funeral is over and the dust has settled, we are eventually alone with God, and the truth about our relationship with Him is unavoidable. Although I had been seeking to walk by faith my entire Christian life, the death of my husband drove

me to develop my trust at a deeper level. That deeper trust
would begin with a new promise.

> Fear not; for thou shalt not be ashamed:
> neither be thou confounded; for thou shalt
> not be put to shame; for thou shalt forget the
> shame of thy youth, and shalt not remember
> the reproach of thy widowhood any more.
> For thy Maker is thine husband; the LORD of
> hosts is his name; and thy Redeemer the Holy
> One of Israel; The God of the whole earth
> shall He be called (Isaiah 54:5–6, KJV).

Don't miss this, ladies! *This is key!* Claim this verse
written specifically for you. In fact, commit it to memory.

When I first read this phrase—"Thy Maker is thine
husband"—I drew comfort from it. As time went on, it
became an immovable anchor in my life. God does not intend
for you to be without the support of a husband when yours
dies. He does not expect your oldest son to take that place,
nor your brother-in-law as in the Old Testament. Don't take
on the load of your husband in addition to your own. God
says plainly and simply, *"I am the man!"* He is, after all, the
Creator God with the entire universe under His authority.
Nothing can happen to us without being filtered through His
divine permission. He has promised to be faithful in all our
circumstances. Take Him seriously.

Have you ever heard, "It's not what you know, but
who you know"? My family always says when you have a
problem, just go to the top, and don't mess around with the
middleman. According to Isaiah 54:4–5, you are married to

the man at the top and there is no one higher. God knows our name and He desires intimacy with us! He is our Redeemer and Savior.

The widow has a special place of protection and privilege in the Lord. He is worthy of our trust. God will challenge you to take Him at His word and, based on my experience, He will deliver. If you feel like you are in that foggy place where everything is all mixed up, it's because God is going to show you how to arrange things differently. If you let Him, He'll help you put it all back. But you can also choose to be angry with Him and refuse to let Him work a better, stronger faith in you.

Looking to God for Answers

Some say women are more verbal than men. I definitely fit that mold. When my husband and I were first married, I would come home from work and follow him around the house, regurgitating my day's activities. I just could not unwind any other way. I remember one time following him into the bathroom. He finally turned to me and said, "Do you mind?" I mention this because many widows struggle, having no one to talk to after their husbands are gone. The one we share most intimately with will secure our trust. We can build a lot of tension inside if we cannot unload verbally, but we must be sensitive about how and to whom we unload. Our teenage children should not be burdened with our emotional releases. It is fine to alert them to issues that will directly impact them, but don't use them as a sounding board.

While family and friends may want to help out with a listening ear, you may find they will have unexpected and sometimes negative reactions to your thoughts and areas of struggle. It may be very hard for them to understand your perspective. We need to understand that we can verbally unload on God. We can shout at the top of our lungs in frustration to Him, or we can laugh and cry with Him. He is there for us, and He has a great sense of humor! He is really the only one who can do anything about our struggle. He knows our minds. He has the resources to fix our problems— financially or otherwise, and He changes hearts. He even has a host of saints at His disposal who are just waiting for an assignment. On whom is it better to depend? God or us? Change the way you think about God.

If you are trying to determine what God wants you to do, pray for His peace. Jeremiah 29:11 says, "For I know the thoughts that I think toward you, saith the Lord, thoughts of peace, and not of evil, to give you an expected end" (KJV). I often hear people say they ask God to close doors to prevent them from making wrong choices. I don't like doors smacking me in the face. You will be better off waiting on God's peace instead of barging into a situation until you are stonewalled. If you are having doubts about a decision, then God hasn't yet given you the go-ahead. It is a good idea not to make any major decisions for the first year of your widowhood. Things will look so different in just a year's time. Some issues will resolve themselves, while others may worsen. Whatever the case, options will be a whole lot clearer a year later.

God provides confirmation of His direction and answers from other sources as well, but the inner peace of heart will bring certainty for action. It is exciting when God is doing something really neat in your life. Embrace it bravely and treat it like an adventure. He has chosen you for reasons of His own. Maybe you do not have an adventurous spirit. Neither did a lot of characters in the Bible, but God had a way of picking them up and setting them on the mark. He can do the same for you.

I had to learn how to look to God for answers because I had never gone to Him seeking interaction. Praying to God and reading His Word had been unrelated practices. He doesn't speak audibly, after all, so I was at a loss to know how to discern His will. It requires practice. Waiting is the secret. God will faithfully respond to your trust. The more you go to Him, the more confident you will be of His answers. Over time you will develop recognition of His non-verbal voice the same way you recognize the voices of your children or friends. If God is providing an answer that you are not hearing, He will speak more loudly. If you try to ignore Him, He will get in your face! Weigh what you believe He is saying against His Word. This is the point of interaction between praying and meditating on His Word. Ask yourself, *Is this direction or answer consistent with biblical principles?* Don't worry if you feel like you don't know the Bible well enough. Begin to read it daily as God calls you, and ask Him to show you what you need to know. He will not fail your trust.

God's Resources

One day I discovered there was not enough money to pay our health insurance premium. I knew we couldn't do without the insurance, and I decided to let God take care of this problem. I committed myself to praying and waiting to see what He would do. He had promised to be my husband, and if my husband were still living, I would go to him with a problem like this. I decided I would not share this need with anyone. Instead I would totally trust His provision.

The days passed and the due date was fast approaching. Two or three days before the bill was due, I went to the mailbox, and there was the total amount needed for the health insurance plus some change. It came from a one-year-old death benefit. I have no idea why I should have received that payment at that particular time—except God. I know when He answers your need, it will be in the most creative and unexpected ways.

Always make prayer your first step, and then wait. Waiting is the most critical step but by far the hardest. I used to hate waiting, but there is safety in waiting on God. Waiting provides time to hear Him speak peace to us, time for Him to put things into place, and time to receive information from Him about how to proceed. God told Isaiah in 55:9, "For as the heavens are higher than the earth, So are my ways higher than your ways, And my thoughts than your thoughts." God wants to observe our hearts during the waiting to discern whether we will try to control the circumstances ourselves. He wants to know we are going to believe Him and allow Him to act on our behalf.

Now, of course, it is just like God both to give a precious nugget of truth and to direct circumstances as we put that truth into practice. Most often the truths God gives us in trials need to be tested in later life experiences. Normally, one must practice something a number of times before it becomes a habit. Trusting God in everything must become a natural reaction, and it can become a habit only with repetition. Therefore, expect trials to come in multiples for the proving of your faith.

God Cares about Details

It is often not difficult for us to trust God in the big things. They are easy to recognize and usually force us to stop. But it's the little, unresolved daily details that build up and unsettle us the most. We try to take care of them ourselves but the next thing we know, we are alone and headed in the wrong direction. Before, we would have complained to our husbands about these problems because, when unaddressed, they often pile up until one precipitates a crisis. By itself, the crisis is not really the problem, but it is the tipping point. How small a problem can we take to the Lord? Does He really want to know about every little detail? Any problem consuming our time and energy that we can't solve on our own belongs to Him. Counting hairs is pretty insignificant in the larger scheme of things, but evidently God doesn't see it that way. Matthew 10:30 tells us that He knows how many hairs are on our heads.

Here is an example. I was just drained of energy when I walked in the door late one afternoon only to meet my teen-age daughter who informed me that there was a "serious problem in the bathroom." We had recently moved into a new home and the toilet in this bathroom had repeatedly overflowed. I thought the problem had been fixed after paying a plumber to snake out the drains.

I had taught my kids what to do if a flushing problem should occur, but somehow in that moment of panic when you realize that the water is rising toward you, your first reaction is to flee. And flee she did—to the hall closet where she retrieved all thirty of my good bath towels, which were now lying on the bathroom floor like water carpet. What a mess! She further informed me that she had attempted to use the plunger to no avail. She had even tried scooping out some of the excess water with the Rubbermaid bowl I use for making cookie dough.

Realizing there was no husband to deal with this, I rolled up my sleeves, stood on the toilet rim to get full leverage and began plunging. The clog was not budging! My daughter seemed unaffected by this problem and was disrespectful at best. When she confessed that she had "accidentally" been flushing some personal feminine items, my unwillingness to excuse her forgetfulness resulted in her further irritation.

I decided I could not deal with this on my own. I would plead with God to fulfill His promise to be my husband in this situation. I called my teenager into the bathroom and told her we were going to pray. I further told her that because of her attitude and irresponsible behavior, she could lead off. She said adamantly, "I am not praying over this toilet!" I replied that she would either get a repentant heart very quickly or

I would immediately call the plumber. A weekend service call to pull the toilet and snake the pipes would cost her a minimum of $125. She prayed, "Dear Lord…"

After her heartfelt confession, I prayed from my heart that God would intervene in this very real problem—to be the husband for me that He had promised to be. After all, He did say in Isaiah 59:1 that His "hand is not so short That it cannot save; Nor is His ear so dull that it cannot hear." I figured it would take a pretty long arm to wrestle with this, and by now I was almost in tears. But God was so faithful! When we finished praying, I reached over and flushed the toilet. To my delight the water flushed as if nothing was wrong, and we haven't had a problem since.

Don't tell me that God doesn't care about the little things. If He will stoop to plunge a toilet, there is no end to what He will do when we call upon Him. If you are the skeptic who says it was the plunging that really did the trick and not the faithful hand of God, you have not yet learned the difference between coincidence and faith.

We can learn to see every experience in life either as part of a plan by a faithful God or just luck and coincidences along the way. One day I was running errands and needed to stop to eat. I was silently praying and thanking God for the great day and the food I was about to eat. I pulled up to the fast food line and placed my order. As I approached the window to pay, I realized I did not have one cent in my purse. I was embarrassed and apologized to the attendant for my error, attempting to cancel the order. He looked at me and smiled. "That's okay. Today's order is on us." Whoa! I couldn't believe it! I call that "the day the Lord took me to lunch." I could have viewed it as nothing more than a nice coincidence, but I know God better than that. He treats me to special occurrences like that all the time, and I give Him the thanks and credit.

God's Purposes

God is the God of the impossible. If our God can provide only those solutions we can imagine, He is too small. We must commit to Him the things we know we cannot solve. If we don't believe He can manage them, how can we trust Him with our salvation?

These experiences have changed my concept of God. Occasionally I hear someone say we must not become so familiar with God that He becomes our "buddy." *We might lose our reverence and respect for Him as God.* But I have found that the more intimate and familiar I become with God as I lean on Him, the more I respect His sovereignty and trust His faithfulness. God is never offended by trust on any level.

I once had the opportunity to help an older widow who had undergone surgery. She had been a widow for less than a year, and when she found out I was also a widow, we began to compare notes. She was still in the early stages of shock and unbelief, and commented that she didn't feel there was anything left to live for. In other words, "My plans have been interrupted and I don't like it, so I'm not moving." I couldn't stop thinking about her attitude. I tried to remember how I got past that point. When we lose our husbands and our world is turned upside down, we are forced to a screeching halt. We cannot pretend that nothing has happened, and it would be unhealthy to try. While we are in this waiting room of time, let's think about the reality of life and eternity.

Our shock is not so much from losing our husbands as from realizing we had been on a life course that did not include this event. It was not on our map. Can you imagine using a map that was taking you to a destination not in your plans? What a surprise that would be! You would wonder, "What happened?"

I easily get lost when driving my car and have scratched my head on more than one occasion, asking, "What did I do wrong?" We sometimes do that with our life course. We think we have been in tune with God's plan, but are we really? Are we sure that we have not followed a plan that seems good to us and merely invited God to come along? As Solomon said, "The mind of man plans his way, But the LORD directs his steps" (Proverbs 16:9). Why are we surprised and sometimes angry to find God in control of the destination?

When I was a little girl, my family would occasionally get into the car and start on a trip just for fun. When we asked my mother where we were going, she would say, "Oh, it's a surprise." We would try to guess, using clues along the way. The fun was not knowing the anticipated destination. The stops along the way did not bother us even if the road took us only to the store to pick up a few things. Usually we ended up getting ice cream or doing some other fun activity.

Jeremiah says in 29:11, "'For I know the plans that I have for you,' declares the LORD, 'plans for welfare and not for calamity to give you a future and a hope.'" We may be surprised by this turn in the road, but God isn't. It was on His map all along. Becoming a widow is not punishment from God. He doesn't stick us with pins to see how much we can take. Don't let Satan lie to you about what has happened. I don't want to oversimplify it, but this is just one of the stops on the map. God has a different destination in mind for you, and because we know He always has our best at heart, we can trust His leading. It will take some time to get over your loss, but you must pick yourself up and take another look at the map. You will find that you have been called to this new season for a new life purpose. Don't dread it. Be excited and energized for it as God mightily works in you.

The Journey of Trust

Remember Moses? God intervened in his life in unexpected ways. After a quick escape from the first forty years with Pharaoh, Moses fled to Midian where he tended sheep another forty years. And God really rocked his world there! These seasons were necessary to prepare Moses for God's ultimate plan—to free the Israelites. God dramatically changed Moses' life experiences three separate times, each forty years apart!

So, when changes in life occur, we must recognize that it's not the end of life; it's merely a transition. You can choose to make your transition miserable, or you can look at it as a trip to a surprise destination. I avoid too much long-term planning in exchange for a more spontaneous and interesting trip. We don't have to know all the details of the journey. We just need to stick close to the guy with the map.

As you begin to respond to this interactive, personal trust in God, you will discover a new personal identity unfolding. It will be a better you, one confident in Christ and one stepping out to live life as you never have before. You may find God calling you to a completely different style—one stripped of everything familiar. Seek Him more than ever before. You will find yourself with Christ in a testimony that becomes a shining light to everyone around you.

Trusting God—really trusting Him—is the most incredible journey you will ever choose to take. The end is freedom. If you previously trusted your husband to manage details and make decisions, you will not be accustomed to trusting God without your husband as the middleman.

In the next chapter we will discuss some of the specific ways we can give control to the Lord. The key is to take authority over our thoughts. The battleground of the mind is where Satan engages us in conflict and where we must surrender to Christ for victory.

Study Guide
Chapter 4: A Twist on Trust
(See page vi for instructions for using the study guide.)

1. What Bible truths have you identified in this chapter as precious promises from Christ for you to believe?

2. What are the key verses that have had a special impact for you? Your ring of verses should be really growing by now. As you meditate on God's Word daily, begin to make a habit of freely adding those verses that speak to your heart. No doubt, these verses have already become a valued source of comfort and encouragement.

3. Trusting in God is a mental exercise. List all the personal circumstances that you are currently struggling with. Pray over each one and release it to God; let Him deal with it. Ask God for direction and intervention and wait. (That's the hard part!) In the days and weeks ahead, every time it comes to mind, pray and release it again. Do not allow yourself to spend time thinking about it. If God wants you to act on it, He will make it very clear, but you must stop holding on mentally.

4. Going back to the list you created above, think about the God-centered perspective you should have with each one. Identify how you can choose not only to stop thinking about those things, but also how you can change the expectations you have for each one. God's ways are not our ways. If you have expectations for how God

will answer each one, you might miss His answer. To change thinking habits, you must plan ahead about what thoughts you will substitute. You are in control of what you think and you need to take responsibility for that. When you change what you think, it in turn will change what you do.

Additional study sheets can be accessed at **www.widowtowidow.net** in Chapter Four under the Study Guide Tab on subjects such as:

- Intimacy with Christ
- Loving God as He wants to be Loved.

Chapter 5

Fight Or Fright
Elements of Spiritual Warfare

❧

Leaning, Not Leading

As widows experiencing one of the most difficult trials of our lives, we need to tap into the power and peace the Lord intends for us. Otherwise, we will become like a fearful, injured animal striving to survive in the wild. Our enemy, Satan, will try to use our circumstances to discourage us and destroy our faith. But the Lord does not intend for us to be defeated.

When my daughter was very young, she would try to walk across our neighbor's field to visit her little friend. About halfway there, a large dog would jump out from his yard and bark at her so forcefully that she would run home in tears. She was convinced the dog was going to eat her alive! I finally told her, "When that big old dog starts to bark at you, in a really brave voice say, 'No, Stormy, you go home!' When he sees you are not afraid of him, he will leave you alone."

Convinced this tactic would work, she boldly started out. True to form, that big old dog came lunging out at her, but when Hilary commanded him in her biggest, bravest voice, the dog went running home as if chased with a stick! She was surprised and delighted! Never again was she afraid to cross that field. What made the difference? The dog hadn't changed, and Hilary was still the same little girl. But she had been empowered by a new understanding of the rules of engagement. No one had told her it could be that easy.

When the reality of my husband's death had settled in, I was so bound in my own set of what seemed to be insurmountable circumstances that I did not know how to manage. As I struggled desperately to move forward with my life, I tried to make everything happen like it should. Going on as if everything was under control and trying to be all things to all people, however, just wasn't working. I was trying too hard to be a brave testimony for the Lord from my own strength.

One day someone from my church looked at me after a long afternoon of trying to keep our five-acre place running and in repair. He said, "You don't have to take a warrior's position in the front lines, Kristine. You are a woman and that is all God expects you to be. Let Him go ahead, and you just follow."

It was some of the best advice anyone has ever given me, and I have never forgotten it. I was trying to patch and fix everything that seemed wrong. I was trying to be the strength of my husband for everyone who needed him. I was trying to lead instead of leaning on the Lord. I didn't understand how He could help me with all of this. My God was too small, and there was a lot I didn't know about the enemy's tactics and efforts to bring my faith to defeat. I had options I wasn't aware of—a hidden cupboard full of tools that had never needed to be opened. As I tearfully prayed, the Lord began to show me things that have taken me to a place of victory. I have learned that it is not His plan for me to be in control. It is God's task to be in control. It is our job to follow His plan.

Unhealthy Emotions

Books have been written about how to work through the stages of grief. I have tried to look at my struggles from a spiritual perspective and have highlighted what I think are the biggest obstacles to recovery. As we deal with our grief and loss and experience the anger and anxiety that accompany them, we are often in and out of depression. We may not even realize we are going through these phases, or if we do, we don't know how to treat them short of medication. I also frequently sensed a presence of evil around me—especially at night. I kept trying but failed to find some semblance of control. There were too many variables that would not line up! What had worked before just didn't work anymore.

The Lord began to remind me of some things I had learned a few years earlier about goal setting that really seemed to apply now. In *Stomping out the Darkness,* Neil Anderson and Dave Park write of three degrees of emotion that should be a thermometer "designed to alert us of poor goals or faulty beliefs."[1] These emotions can easily become the tail that wags the dog. The emotions are anger, anxiety, and depression. The authors explain how these feelings can expose the goals we have set, and why that is so important to understand.

Anger

> When you're feeling angry about a relationship or a project, it's usually because someone or something has blocked your goal. Any goal that can be blocked by forces you can't control (other than God) *is not a healthy goal* because your success is out of your hands…Feelings of anger warn us to reexamine what we believe and the goals we have put together.[2]

The Lord tells us to "be angry, and yet do not sin; do not let the sun go down on your anger, and do not give the devil an opportunity" (Ephesians 4:26–27). James says in 1:19–20, "But let everyone be quick to hear, slow to speak and slow to anger." We are to release our anger quickly and not let a bitter root take hold.

When we are angry, we need to stop to identify the goal that has been frustrated. It will most likely be a goal that involves others. Mothers, for example, are often guilty of setting goals for their children. Rather than setting goals for them, however, it is better to determine that we will be the best mom we can be or that we will be the best godly witness we can be in their lives. These are goals that are in our control. God can use them to influence our children and their walk.

Anxiety

> When we feel anxious in an activity or
> relationship, our anxiety may be signaling that
> we're not sure about the goal we have chosen.
> We hope something will happen, but we have
> no guarantee that it will. We can control some
> of the factors, but not all of them, so worry
> begins to chew at our insides.[3]

When you are anxious or worrying, stop to identify the
goal. Ask God to help you let go of everything that involves
other parties. Set a new goal that involves only you and the
part you play in this concern. Focus exclusively on that. Do
not let yourself be involved at any other level. Those concerns
that do not fit into your sphere of allowable control must be
entrusted to the Lord. Let God bless you with the peace that
comes from letting go. Being in control of yourself and your
relationship with God will be enough for this life.

Depression

> When we base our future success on
> something that can never happen, we have
> an impossible, hopeless goal. Depression is
> a signal that our goal, no matter how spiritual
> or noble, may never be reached. Depression
> is the expression of hopelessness.[4]

As we reevaluate our goals remember that "…whatever
is not from faith is sin" (Rom. 14:23). No matter what you

are doing, if you are not trusting God for it, it is sin. We must be in a continual attitude of prayer and waiting on the Lord for all our decisions and directions. This may not be your regular pattern. It will take some time and practice, and you will make mistakes. Count on it! But God will be faithful if you trust Him. He will help you begin to think about things in a different way.

Anderson and Park go on to say,

> A *godly goal* is any specific choice reflecting God's purposes for your life that does not depend on people or circumstances beyond your ability or right to control. Who do you have the ability and right to control? Virtually no one but yourself. The only person who can block a godly goal or render it uncertain or impossible is you. And if you adopt the attitude of cooperation with God's goals… your goal can be reached.[5]

In goal setting, let us practice faithfully Proverbs 16:3 that says, "Commit your works to the LORD, and your plans will be established."

Once God reminded me of these truths, I began to use these emotions as a warning flag alerting me to reevaluate what I was attempting. Instead of these emotions continuing to control me, they became a useful tool to get me back on track.

Fear

Fear is never from God. "For God hath not given us the spirit of fear; but of power, and of love, and of a sound mind"

(2 Tim. 1:7, KJV). Fear should be a red flag alerting us that we have allowed Satan to take ground in our mind. Satan, as a created being, is not omniscient. He is unable to read our minds, but fear is a tactic he uses effectively to put thoughts into our minds. He may even use these thoughts to condemn our godly character. The thoughts may be unbelievably wicked or frightening. Many times they are the source of anxiety because they capitalize on our unhealthy goals and may later make us captive to various phobias and emotional attacks.

Discouragement

Another bump that seems to place itself in the road at times is discouragement. According to Merriam Webster's Collegiate® Dictionary, discouragement means "to deprive of courage or confidence."[6] Smith writes, "The power of temptation is in the fainting of our own hearts."[7] If Satan can accomplish this cowering of our spirits in discouragement, then his next victory will be our fall to temptation and sin. Seven times in the book of Joshua God tells Joshua to take courage and not be afraid because God would bring the victory to enter the Promised Land. If we are trusting God for the plan He has set before us, we cannot fail.

Avoiding Satan's Deception

Second Corinthians 10:4–5 says, "For the weapons of our warfare are not of the flesh, but divinely powerful for the destruction of fortresses. We are destroying speculations and every lofty thing raised up against the knowledge of God, and we are taking every thought captive to the obedience of

Christ." We need to take control of our minds by trusting the Lord through prayer and meditating on His Word. This will bring the Lord powerfully to our aid.

Another way to check our thoughts is to claim Jeremiah 29:11: "'I know the thoughts that I think toward you,' saith the LORD, 'thoughts of peace, and not of evil, to give you an expected end'" (KJV). The test then becomes whether or not the thought is bringing spiritual peace and is consistent with His Word. If it doesn't, then it is not of God.

Don't let yourself board that runaway thought train. The path is torturous and unnecessary. Most of the time the worst scenarios we can imagine never come to pass, but the thought of their possibility can cripple us. It places us in a paralyzing state of spiritual bondage, rendering us ineffective for the cause of Christ. That is Satan's goal. Not bringing our thoughts under control will cause stress and rob us of energy. Do not let Satan deceive you in this area.

The Presence of Evil

Feeling the presence of evil is related, in part, to fear. As believers in Christ we should know the authority we have to cast evil away from our presence. Paul reveals to us in Colossians that God created more than what is visible in this material world. The good news is that everything He creates is under His total authority and power. "And in Him you have been made complete, and He is the head over all rule and authority" (Col. 2:10). "For in Him [Christ] all things were created, both in the heavens and on earth, visible and invisible, whether thrones or dominions or rulers or authorities—all things have been created through Him and for Him. And He is before all things" (Col. 1:16, 17). He also tells us in Col. 1:13 that if we are in Christ, we have been "delivered…from the domain of darkness."

If you are experiencing a sense of evil presence, you need to speak out loud that you are a child of God and that Jesus Christ is your Lord and Savior. In the name of Jesus Christ and by His authority, demand that this presence be gone now. If you belong to Christ, the presence cannot stand against His name, nor does it want to. This is often referred to as binding the enemy. "Submit therefore to God. Resist the devil and he will flee from you. Draw near to God and He will draw near to you" (James 4:7–8).

Letting Go

One of the most difficult areas for me as a widow has been learning how to let go of things. Friends had told me to trust God with my concerns and then lay them down, but it didn't seem to work for me. One day I picked up a book entitled, *The Christian's Secret of a Happy Life,* by Hannah Whitall Smith. I found help in chapter three, "The Life Defined."

She refers to our Christian life as the "life hid with Christ in God" and says that

> its chief characteristics are an entire surrender to the Lord and a perfect trust in Him, resulting in victory over sin, and inward rest of soul; and it differs from the lower range of Christian experience in that

it causes us to let the Lord carry our burdens and manage our affairs for us, instead of trying to do it ourselves.

Most Christians are like a man who was toiling along the road, bending under a heavy burden, when a wagon overtook him, and the driver kindly offered to help him on his journey. He joyfully accepted the offer, but when seated in the wagon, continued to bend beneath his burden, which he still kept on his shoulders. "Why do you not lay down your burden?" asked the kind-hearted driver. "Oh" replied the man, "I feel that it is almost too much to ask you to carry me, and I could not think of letting you carry my burden too." And so Christians, who have given themselves into the care and keeping of the Lord Jesus, still continue to bend beneath the weight of their burdens, and often go weary and heavy-laden throughout the whole length of their journey.[8]

We must discover the practice of making godly goals and leaving the rest with the Lord. It will really lighten our burden. Expounding on this idea, Smith also writes of a tract entitled "Hannah's Faith." It is the story of

a poor woman who had been carried triumphantly through a life of unusual sorrow. She was giving the history of her life to a kind

visitor on one occasion, and at the close the
visitor said feelingly "Oh, Hannah, I do not
see how you could bear so much sorrow!" "I
did not bear it," was the quick reply; "the Lord
bore it for me." "Yes," said the visitor, "that
is the right way. We must take our troubles
to the Lord." "Yes," replied Hannah, "but we
must do more than that: we must *leave* them
there. Most people," she continued, "take
their burdens to Him, but they bring them
away with them again, and are just as worried
and unhappy as ever. But I take mine, and I
leave them with Him, and come away and
forget them. If the worry comes back, I take
it to Him again; and I do this over and over,
until at last I just forget I have any worries,
and am at perfect rest."[9]

To be sure, this involves our believing that the Lord is
taking what we give Him without any strings attached. We
can't say, "Now Lord, I am giving this to you, but this is
what I expect You to do with it," and then keep watching it.
We have to let go completely and walk away.

You can count on Satan slipping it back into your mind,
though. He hopes you won't repeat the giving up process
again, but you must. Repeat it over and over for as many
times as it takes until it is finally gone from your thinking.
In this way we can abandon our whole self to the Lord along
with every trouble we have. It is as simple as believing God.
Do you really believe Him? The circumstance may not

change, but that is not your concern. God will deal with that. You will receive the peace that comes with the simple trust of leaving it with Him.

Hope for Success

Remember Gideon? God called him to deliver Israel from Midian. In Gideon's discouragement, he cried, "Oh my lord, if the LORD is with us, why then has all this happened to us? And where are all His miracles which our fathers told us about, saying, 'Did not the LORD bring us up from Egypt?' But now the LORD has abandoned us and given us into the hand of Midian" (Judges 6:13).

Maybe you feel like you have been delivered into the hands of the Midianites. Your heart has fainted from lack of confidence, and yet God calls you to go forward. Just as He said to Gideon, He says to you, "Go in this your strength and deliver Israel from the hand of Midian. *Have I not sent you?"* (Judges 6:14, emphasis added).

Has not God Himself saved you for this plan? You must trust Him for it. You can either go forward in the power and strength of the Lord because you believe Him, or wade through in your own strength. Do not let a faint heart stop you. Victory is just a step away.

As we consider spiritual warfare, we must first identify our enemy. Satan is the enemy that attacks us. We might wonder why he hates us so much and seems determined to break us. It is because we remind him of our Creator. We are created in God's image, and Satan hates God. He defeated Satan at the cross and set him as Christ's footstool. We are created in the likeness of this One who has thwarted Satan's ambition to reign and be worshiped. This enemy does not want us to know the truth because it would set us free. He will do everything he can to get us off track. We must guard our hearts, stay grounded in the Word of God, and put our complete trust in the Lord Jesus alone.

As the enemy seeks to break us, it is in the areas of anger, anxiety, depression, evil presence, worry, and discouragement that he can gain the strongest hold. We must identify an important tactic if we are to gain advantage in these six areas. That tactic is to believe Christ and seek a oneness of mind with Him. It is oneness with Christ that equips us to make the right choice deliberately. In contrast to deliberate choice, how many times have you said, "I will *try*"? It's almost like saying, "I will make the effort but I don't expect much to change." That sounds like defeat even before you start. It's not deliberate or purposeful. Hannah Whitall Smith has some important thoughts concerning our will in chapter 7 of *The Christian's Secret of a Happy Life.*

> The common thought is that this life hid with Christ in God is to be lived in the emotions, and consequently all the attention of the soul is directed toward them, and as they are satisfactory or otherwise, the soul rests or is troubled. Now, the truth is, that this life is not to be lived in the emotions at all, but in the will; and therefore, if only the will is kept steadfastly abiding in its center, God's will,

the varying states of emotion do not in the least disturb or affect the reality of the life.

By the will I do not mean the wish of the man, or even his purpose, but the deliberate choice, the deciding power, the king, to which all that is in the man must yield obedience. It is the man, in short, the *ego*, that which we feel to be ourselves.

For the decisions of our will are often so directly opposed to the decisions of our emotions, that, if we are in the habit of considering our emotions as the test, we shall be very apt to feel like hypocrites in declaring those things to be real which our will alone had decided. But the moment we see that the will is king, we shall utterly disregard anything that clamors against it, and shall claim as real its decisions, let the emotions rebel as they may. I am aware that this is a difficult subject to deal with; but it is so exceedingly practical in its bearing upon the life of faith that I beg of you, dear reader, not to turn from it until you have mastered it.

Your part then is simply to put your will, in this matter of believing, over on God's side, making up your mind that you will believe what He says, because He says it, and that you will not pay any regard to the feelings that make it seem so unreal. God will not fail to respond, sooner or later, with his revelation to such a faith.

The secret lies just here—that our will, which is the spring of all our actions, has been in the past under the control of sin and self, and these have worked in us all their own good pleasure. But now God calls upon us to yield our wills up to Him, that He may take control of them, and may work in us to will and to do of His good pleasure. If we will obey this call, and present ourselves to Him as a living sacrifice, He will take possession of our surrendered wills, and will begin at once to work in us "'that which is well-pleasing in His sight, through Jesus Christ,' giving us the mind that was in Christ, and transforming us into His image (see Rom. 12:1–2).

For God can only carry out His own will with us as we consent to it, and will in harmony with Him.

He wills that you should be entirely surrendered to Him, and that you should trust Him perfectly.[10]

The Armor of God

Finally, this chapter would not be complete without including the Lord's instructions concerning the powerful armor He has provided for our spiritual battle. This armor is the secret weapon hidden in the cupboard I wrote of earlier— armor you might not have known you possessed. Beginning in Ephesians 6:11, Paul tells us how to use this armor as we stand against the wiles of the devil. Know first, however, that this spiritual battle is unseen with human eyes. Second, that we have authority in Christ because He sits at the right hand of God the Father in the heavenly places with all rule and authority at His feet. Satan is a defeated foe.

Helmet of Salvation

This important piece protects our mind where the battle takes place. The spiritual battle is one of thought and choice controlled by our will. Symbolically, the helmet is our salvation. Chapter two explained in detail how to receive that salvation. Salvation and its resulting oneness with Christ give us the advantage we need to control our thoughts where sin originates. So, recognize clearly the helmet of salvation and wear it knowingly.

Breastplate of Righteousness

Righteousness means being right with God. It is not about being a good person or doing good things. God declares us to be righteous when we put our faith in Him. "For what does the Scripture say? 'And Abraham believed God, and it was reckoned to him as righteousness" (Rom. 4:3). Righteousness is possible because of the sacrifice of Christ. "He made Him [Christ] who knew no sin to be sin on our behalf, that we might become the righteousness of God in

Him" (2 Cor. 5:21). Because of righteousness, sin has no power to send us to hell. This powerful piece of armor called righteousness is given to us as we enter into Christ at salvation. It is unchangeable, but Satan will try to convince us that we are unrighteous before God. He wants us to cower before God. Let us not lose our confidence in Christ because of Satan's lies.

Belt of Truth

"And you will know the truth, and the truth will make you free" (John 8:32). Jesus also said, "I am the way, and the truth, and the life; no one comes to the Father, but through me" (John 14:6). Our enemy, Satan, cannot come against us without first facing the authority of Christ in us. It is this position of authority that empowers us through prayer against his attacks. Nothing can come to us unless Christ has allowed it, and He will be with us in it. We must trust Him even when it doesn't make sense. The knowledge of this trust is our freedom.

Feet Shod with the Gospel

Our feet are "…shod…with the preparation of the gospel of peace" (Eph. 6:15). Isaiah writes in 52:7:

> How lovely on the mountains
> Are the feet of him who brings good news,
> Who announces peace
> And brings good news of happiness,
> Who announces salvation,
> And says to Zion, "Your God reigns!"

Chapter 5

As we spread the message of salvation with our personal testimony, we light up the world. Because of the good news, Satan's plan becomes greatly compromised.

Shield of Faith

Faith is another piece of defensive armor in our other hand. "In addition to all, taking up the shield of faith with which you will be able to *extinguish all the flaming missiles of the evil one*" (Eph. 6:16, emphasis added). "Now faith is the assurance of things hoped for, the conviction of things not seen" (Hebrews 11:1). Faith is choosing to believe. If we are going to believe in God, let us believe in Him completely, not only for our salvation but also for His strength that will triumph in spiritual warfare. When David faced the giant Goliath, he did not see him in relationship to himself but in relationship to God. A friend reminds me often, "Don't tell God about the mountain; tell the mountain about God." Faith is our victory. Claim it with boldness.

Sword of the Spirit

In addition to defensive armor, God has provided a powerful weapon for the believer to use offensively in the spiritual warfare he must face. He has placed in our hand the sword of the Spirit, which is the Word of God. Is it powerful? "For the word of God is living and active and sharper than any two-edged sword, and piercing as far as the division of soul and spirit, of both joints and marrow, and able to judge the thoughts and intentions of the heart" (Hebrews 4:12). God communicates His will to our minds through His Word.

Fight or Fright

Because the Bible is the standard used to measure everything in our lives, every decision should be weighed on its scales. It should be the source of our meditation. Our faith grows from its pages. This is the tool the Holy Spirit uses to bring conviction of sin, righteousness, and judgment (John 16:8). Furthermore, it is the Christian's strongest weapon against the lies of Satan. As Jesus used the Scriptures to defeat Satan in His temptation, so we must use the Word to defend our faith and to fight against the spiritual forces of evil.

Prayer

In addition, Paul commands us to pray as we enter this battle. He instructs us, "With all prayer and petition pray at all times in the Spirit, and with this in view be on the alert with all perseverance and petition for all the saints" (Eph. 6:18). Satan works hard against the attitude of prayer. It is often difficult for us to give prayer priority. The Scriptures are full of reminders that prayer is a powerful tool in our hands, yet we often use it for our own purposes and not in the power the Lord intended. James 4:3 says, "You ask and do not receive, because you ask with wrong motives, so that you may spend it on your pleasures." Let us pray "in the Spirit" and "with all perseverance and petition for all saints." Only death or unconsciousness can stop us from talking to the Lord. No one else has to hear us communicating with our Father, but He hears and is faithful to meet our needs.

≈ 91 ≈

The Battle

This spiritual battle will continue until we finally meet the Lord. If we learn to find safety in our spiritual armor, we will be protected. As we take authority in controlling our thoughts, we will find peace and victory. These are the Christian's defining habits. How we think and evaluate our experiences from the mind of Christ is the essence of having our identity in Him. This powerful identity and its elements are the fruit of the life hidden in Christ. This is the God-center from which we as believers must operate. If we can accomplish this through Christ, we will be prepared for the journey ahead.

Study Guide
Chapter 5: Fight or Fright
(See page vi for instructions for using the study guide.)

1. This chapter includes some powerful mental tools! Start by identifying the precious promises from Christ that you can claim and that will deliver victorious results.

2. What are the key verses from this chapter that will help you in the mental battle you are engaged in? Add them to your key ring.

3. Remember that the focus of God's perspective always has to do with His plan for the lost and bringing glory to Himself. Can you begin to look at your circumstances and see that He may be using you for that end? This will require you to get your mind out of a self-centered orientation.

4. In the areas of fear and worry, identify how you will begin to change your thinking patterns. Ask the Holy Spirit to speak to you in a way that helps you recognize when you are taking a ride on the runaway thought train. Plan now how you will train your mind to stop. It may help to think this out on paper.

5. Practice using anger, anxiety, and depression to identify the expectations you have that are ungodly. Write down the specific areas where you are experiencing these emotions right now. List the expectations you have had in the past. Ask God to help you release them. Now make a list of new expectations for each area that only you and God can control. Finally, what is left on this list of expectations that only you can control? Even that may require the help of God's grace.

Several additional study sheets can be accessed at **www.widowtowidow.net** in Chapter Five under the Study Guide Tab on subjects such as:

- Godly goals vs. Ungodly Goals
- Temptation
- The Mental Spiritual Battle
- How the Spiritual Armor (Ephesians 6) Can Be Used.

Chapter 6

Where Is God?

Understanding God's Perspective on Suffering and Death

❧

The subjects of death and suffering are sobering. Most of us prefer to spend time planning and thinking about living, not dying. We become caught up in life on earth as if we will be here forever and often become greedy for the temporary things this life offers. Consequently, our spiritual life may seem gray compared to the brilliant but quickly fading colors of the world around us. Furthermore, we develop a false sense of control. Because we have forgotten life's temporary nature, we are startled when God calls a loved one into eternity. We should be prepared for the inevitable death and suffering that are part of God's plan, but few are ready.

So, what are we to do when death becomes our reality? What eternal perspective should we embrace? It is important to allow time to mourn and grieve the loss of a spouse; it is healthy to do so. There may be days throughout the rest of our lives that will bring tears, but we must not allow our grief to destroy us or become an unquenchable bitterness. The Lord wants to use us, but if we allow ourselves to become mired in our grief, we will be useless for the task for which these experiences were intended to equip us. Satan would like us to respond to our situation as if God had assaulted us personally. Death and suffering will always bring pain, but if we accept them by taking an eternal perspective, they will not defeat us. It all depends on how we choose to respond to our experience.

If we are to gain an understanding of God's perspective, we must go to His Word. We cannot gain the reality of who God is from our imagination, what we have heard about Him, or what we wish Him to be. When someone says, "The God I know would never let something like this happen," it suggests they do not really know God. What the Scriptures say about suffering and death comes from a very different perspective. Let us review some of the passages that present God's viewpoint. There is a great difference between God's allowing an event to happen and His causing the event.

Suffering

Scripture References

> As an example, brethren, of suffering and patience, take the prophets who spoke in the name of the Lord. We count them blessed who

endured. You have heard of the endurance of
Job, and have seen the outcome of the Lord's
dealings, that the Lord is full of compassion
and is merciful (James 5:10–11).

James is telling us to take hope in the example of others
who have suffered and experienced God's mercy. The
twelve apostles, men whom Jesus loved, suffered greatly as
they served the Lord and experienced horrible deaths. They
measured everything against their love for Christ. Life is
a vapor in time—just a breath in the span of eternity. The
closer we become to Christ, the more He will bring us lasting
peace. If thoughts of Him do not bring us peace and comfort,
then we need to examine whether or not our relationship
with Christ is our most important priority.

Now for a little while, if necessary, you have
been distressed by various trials, so that the
proof of your faith, being more precious than
gold which is perishable, even though tested
by fire, may be found to result in praise and
glory and honor at the revelation of Jesus
Christ (1 Peter 1:6–7).

We may think it is our good works that are pleasing to
the Lord, but Peter says it is the proving of our faith that is
more precious to Him than gold. This process can come only
through suffering and trials. It is not our works but the faith
that drives them that interests God. We need to start looking
at our experience from the perspective of what is precious to
God if we are to discover meaning in our circumstances.

"But if when you do what is right and suffer for it you patiently endure it, this finds favor with God. For you have been called for this purpose, since Christ also suffered for you, leaving you an example for you to follow in His steps" (1 Peter 2:20–21). At times we may be more willing to suffer for what is right than for a personal injustice against us, but it is all the same to God. It all builds character and fashions us for the spiritual home that Christ is preparing. If we are to appreciate eternity, we must undergo a spiritual preparation to acquire a taste for it. Suffering is a primary tool in that preparation because it exposes our vulnerabilities and takes us out of our comfort zone.

The Example of Christ

So, how should we handle this interruption of suffering? Consider the example of Christ. What did Christ do when He suffered for the sake of righteousness? "And while being reviled, He did not revile in return; while suffering, He uttered no threats, but kept entrusting Himself to Him who judges righteously" (1 Peter 2:23). We are not perfect like Christ, but that is no excuse for our frail humanity. Christ was human, too. When we suffer, we feel His pain as He did. We understand His sacrifice better. Instead of asking God, "Do you see what I am going through?" our God-centered focus says, "Look what Christ has gone through for me!"

Do you feel pain? Feel it as He felt it. Has anyone spit in *your* face? Begin to look at pain and insult from where He sat and it will change your outlook. Part of Christ's drawing us to Himself includes touching His pain. But be reassured, we will never experience His pain without His presence with us. Although He is with us in our suffering, Christ was abandoned by God in His. In His most agonizing hour, the Lord's own Father turned His back on Him as He carried *our* sin on His bloodied shoulders.

The Bible records in Isaiah 53:10, "But the Lord was pleased to crush Him [Christ], putting Him to grief; if He would render Himself as a guilt offering." In verse 11 Isaiah writes, "As a result of the anguish of His soul, He [God] will see it and be satisfied." If it pleased God to crush Christ on the cross, if it brought satisfaction to Him, can we not begin to look at our own suffering as a means to bring praise and glory to God? It is an opportunity to bring an offering to the very throne of God.

I used to have a cat that was a great hunter and often shared her half-eaten treasures from the field with me. She would leave them on the front porch right outside the door, so I would be sure to find them. This was her way of honoring me with a special gift. She was sure I would appreciate it and had no idea how revolted I was as I tried to quickly put it out of sight. What do we lay at the feet of Jesus as an offering? The Scriptures clearly indicate that God is not looking for good works. Isaiah 64:6 says, "For all of us have become like one who is unclean, and all our righteous deeds are like a filthy garment." God is interested in our obedience, our motives, whom we trust, and what we think as we work through trials.

Just as my cat and I had a different idea of what was a treasure, so we need to get on track with Christ's idea of what is precious and satisfying to His Spirit. It is not our good works but rather a broken and contrite heart that God will not despise (Psalm 51:17). Our suffering then may be an instrument for God's pleasure because it can drive us to our knees in a brokenness that reveals a passionate desire and desperate need for a relationship with Christ. As we offer the gift of our full surrender that comes out of our suffering, we will find a powerful call to relationship with Christ.

Peter writes,

> Beloved, do not be surprised at the fiery ordeal among you which comes upon you for your testing, as though some strange thing were happening to you; but to the degree that you share the sufferings of Christ, keep on rejoicing, so that also at the revelation of His glory, you may rejoice with exultation. If you are reviled for the name of Christ, you are blessed, because the Spirit of glory and of God rests upon you…but if anyone suffers as a Christian, he is not to be ashamed, but is to glorify God…therefore, those also who suffer according to the will of God shall entrust their souls to a faithful Creator in doing what is right" (1 Peter 4:12–14, 16, 19).

As the Scriptures have reiterated all along, the desired reaction to suffering is to trust the Lord through it. The decision to trust Him and not act on our own behalf is the faith builder. Be assured, He is in control of every moment, and your surrender in suffering is an offering to His throne.

Many of these passages from 1 Peter speak about the Christian who is suffering for doing good. In 1 Peter 5:8–10, though, Peter introduces a new twist on the reason for suffering. He writes,

> Be of sober spirit, be on the alert. Your adversary, the devil, prowls about like a roaring lion, seeking someone to devour. But resist him, firm in your faith, knowing that the same experiences of suffering are being accomplished by your brethren who are in the world. And after you have suffered for a little while, the God of all grace, who called you to His eternal glory in Christ, will Himself perfect, confirm, strengthen and establish you.

In this type of trial we need to lean heavily on our spiritual armor, as we learned in chapter five. You might be surprised to think that God would actually allow the enemy to bring an assault against His saints. Remember Job, however. The first three chapters of Job in the Old Testament give insight on how far God may allow Satan to have his way with us and for what purpose he might be *given permission.*

The Example of Job

Job was a righteous man, bringing glory to the Lord by his life. Job 1:1 describes him as "…blameless, upright, fearing God and turning away from evil." In this record, Satan actually goes before the presence of God and challenges Job's righteousness. Satan insists that Job's behavior was only because God's blessing had been upon his life. God then gives Satan permission to alter Job's life, but retains control of the conditions and parameters of this alteration. At no time is Satan in control.

Why, we might ask, would God grant such permission? We know from Scripture that God has promised never to give us more than we can bear. He knew what Job was capable of handling. Through this trial Job became stronger in his faith as he was stretched to practice it. Job's faithfulness to the Lord, as a result of his testing, brought glory and honor to God.

Job makes an interesting comment to his three friends in Job 3:25–26, "For what I fear comes upon me, And what I dread befalls me. I am not at ease, nor am I quiet; And I am not at rest, but turmoil comes." God knows us so intimately. He knows our hopes, our fears, and everything in the secret places of our hearts. It appears that Job was being compromised on some level by a hidden fear. What he feared most, God allowed to happen in his life—not to punish him for fearing but to show him that God is greater than fear. God desires to disable fear.

By faith in God, Job learned that he was able to overcome. Job 1:22 reveals that, "Through all this Job did not sin, nor did he blame God." The one thing Job feared most was finally exposed and forever removed through God's faithfulness to him. The lesson here is not that God will bring into your life what you fear, but that He wants to remove whatever holds us in bondage. The strength and character to overcome may be realized only by suffering and trial. Only God can make that call. And what was the outcome of Job's faith? "The Lord blessed the latter days of Job more than his beginning…And Job died, an old man and full of days" (Job 42:12, 17).

The Example of Joseph

As an example of this principle, Smith looks at the life of Joseph. She writes,

> Take Joseph. What could have seemed more apparently on the face of it to be the result of sin, and utterly contrary to the will of God, than the action of his brethren in selling him into slavery? And yet Joseph, in speaking of it, said, "As for you, ye thought evil against me; but God meant it unto good. Now therefore be not grieved, nor angry with yourselves, that ye sold me hither: for God did send me before you to preserve life." It was undoubtedly sin in Joseph's brethren, but by the time it had reached Joseph it had become God's will for him, and was, in truth, though he did not see it then, the greatest blessing of his whole life. And thus we see how God can make even "the wrath of man to praise Him," and how all things, even the sins of others, "shall work together for good to them that love him."[1]

Can you apply that to your life? Can you re-examine your suffering and see God in it? If you can, you will at least be free from the bondage and bitterness of it, and by faith you will be able to receive it and bear its burden with understanding. You will bring glory to God with such a testimony.

Chapter 6

God Is in Control

Whether our trials come while we are doing what is right, from the attacks of Satan, or as the result of sin, God is in control and has a plan for our good in them. Hannah Whitall Smith in *The Christian's Secret of a Happy Life* shares insight about God's full control of the events of our lives. She writes,

> For nearly everything in life comes to us through human instrumentality, and most of our trials are the result of somebody's failure, or ignorance, or carelessness, or sin. We know God cannot be the author of these things; and yet, unless He is the agent in the matter, how can we say to Him about it, "Thy will be done?"[2]

> What is needed, then, is to see God in everything, and to receive everything directly from His hands, with no intervention of second causes; and it is to just this that we must be brought, before we can know an abiding experience of entire abandonment and perfect trust … To the children of God, everything comes directly from their Father's hand, no matter who or what may have been the apparent agents. There are no "second causes" for them.[3]

> Second causes must all be under the control of our Father, and not one of them can touch

us except with His knowledge and by His permission. It may be the sin of man that originates the action, and therefore the thing itself cannot be said to be the will of God; but by the time it reaches us it has become God's will for us, and must be accepted as directly from His hands. No man or company of men, no power in earth or heaven, can touch that soul which is abiding in Christ, without first passing through His encircling presence, and receiving the seal of his permission. If God be for us, it matters not who may be against us; nothing can disturb or harm us, except He shall see that it is best for us, and shall stand aside to let it pass.[4]

Death

Now, move to another difficult reality—death. Everyone living in this world should expect death. It is either an unwelcome stranger or an expected guest. For every widow reading this book, death has been a familiar presence. We should be making different preparations for its next visit unless we were wise enough to be prepared for the first one. Psalm 139:16 says, "And in your book were all written, The days that were ordained for me, When as yet there was not one of them." The time of our departure is surer to the Lord than the human prediction of our birth.

That might seem odd to us living here in time, but God is outside of time. He knows every decision we will make, not because He controls our decisions, but because He knows the beginning from the end. So our days are numbered from the start. Death is not a punishment but a running out of the clock for this earthly life—a last breath that is not divinely extended. The limited time we were given in God's purpose for us on earth is over.

Solomon tells us in the third chapter of Ecclesiastes that there is a season for every event under heaven. There is a season to die, a season to weep, and a season to mourn. When Jesus stood at the grave of His beloved friend Lazarus and witnessed the grief of Mary and all those that loved Lazarus, "He was deeply moved in spirit, and was troubled" (John 11:33). Verse 35 says, "Jesus wept." From our finite perspective we assume that He was sad that Lazarus was dead. Yet in John 11: 6, 17, and 30 it is clear that Jesus was intentionally tarrying in going to Lazarus. He said in John 11:4, "This sickness is not to end in death, but for the glory of God, so that the Son of God may be glorified by it." Why would He be weeping if He knew that He was going to raise Lazarus from the dead for the glory of God?

I believe that Jesus, in His humanity, felt compassion for Mary and the other Jews as He witnessed their obvious grief. Could it also be that His sorrow was over a world that struggled to understand who He was because it could not accept Him as God? They still did not see the spiritual side of the picture. Perhaps His sorrow was that He needed to call Lazarus back from the peace and presence of God to return to a world lost in sin.

Psalm 116:15 says, "Precious in the sight of the Lord is the death of His godly ones." Solomon writes in Ecclesiastes 7:1, "A good name is better than a good ointment; and the day of one's death is better than the day of one's birth." In verse 8 he says again, "The end of a matter is better than its beginning." We might ask ourselves, "What kind of a God finds *pleasure* in physical death?" The answer is a God who is Spirit, a God who stands outside of time in anticipation and excitement, awaiting the arrival of His beloved ones. We mourn over this physical world and the losses we experience in it while we question God, His wisdom, and the plan that allows these things to happen. Yet we forget that God is Spirit and, made in His image, so are we. Our spirit is what God is focused on and what His plan is all about.

We must realize that death is a result of man's sin nature. For God said in the garden, "But from the tree of the knowledge of good and evil you shall not eat, for in the day that you eat from it you will surely die" (Genesis 2:17). And now we do have the knowledge of good and evil. God moved man away from the tree of life so he would not eat and live forever (see Genesis 3:22–23). But we will see that tree again on either side of the river of life, bearing fruit in the new heaven and earth that the Lord has gone to prepare for us (see Revelation 21:1, 22:1–2). That is where our focus should be.

Since we are visitors here, we must be ready at any minute to leave for home. That's a different perspective from the world's. Our physical body, as we know it, is temporary and inefficient. When Jesus returns for believers, our bodies will be transformed, and we will be joined to a spiritual body in the same way as Christ is joined to His for eternity.

> There is one fate for all men…the hearts of the sons of men are full of evil and insanity is in their hearts throughout their lives. Afterwards they go to the dead…. For the living know they will die; but the dead do not know anything, nor have they any longer a reward, for their memory is forgotten. Indeed their love, their hate and their zeal have already perished, and they will no longer have a share in all that is done under the sun (Ecclesiastes 9:3, 5–6).

Finally, 2 Corinthians 5:1–10 reveals the frailty of this human shell described by Paul as an earthly tent. As we are being torn from this tent in death, a spiritual groaning occurs. When the Lord took my husband that early June morning, there was a point when I was able to witness this separation taking place. I could sense my husband's struggle with leaving his earthly tent and all that he loved here, to be released into the presence of Christ. It is a mystery and a great unknown that Paul explains in 2 Corinthians 5:5–9,

> Now He who prepared us for this very purpose is God, who gave to us the Spirit as a pledge. Therefore, being always of good courage, and knowing that while we are at home in the body we are absent from the Lord—for we walk by faith, not by sight—we are of good courage, I say, and prefer rather to be absent from the body

and to be at home with the Lord. Therefore we also have as our ambition, whether at home or absent, to be pleasing to Him.

It will be like Christmas morning when we enter into the presence of our Lord and He showers us with the rewards of our works that have passed the test of fire. No doubt we will wish we had done more, but just to be united with Him in His glorious presence will be enough.

Is Christ enough for you today—enough to devote your life to Him? Do you find Him sufficient for every moment, every struggle, every joy? What about that glorious mansion He has prepared that is so vividly described at the end of Revelation? How can we look at death with unending anger, tears, and mourning when we know what great joy and splendor our loved ones in Christ are experiencing? How can we not celebrate joyously when in the twinkling of an eye, we will be there, too! Are you getting ready to go? Are you busy doing everything the Lord wants you to finish before He calls you? I hope so because in God's eternity there is a party goin' on, and you've been invited!

Study Guide
Chapter 6: Where Is God?
(See page vi for instructions for using the study guide.)

1. What Bible truths have you identified as precious promises from Christ for you to believe and act on that relate specifically to the themes of death and suffering?

2. List the key verses that have spoken to you and add them to your key ring.

3. As you review the themes of this chapter, mentally note or write down how your view of death and of suffering may have been different from God's view. I hope the truths you have learned about His perspective have brought peace to your heart and a more comfortable way of thinking about these difficult areas.

4. What have you identified in the context of this chapter that you need to begin thinking differently about? Write down the specific steps you will take to change what you think and your actions.

5. You may need to re-evaluate some of your expectations in the areas of death and suffering. If this is the case, make a list of the godly goals that are more appropriate and will bring peace to your struggle.

Part Three:

Season Of Sufficiency

Chapter 7

Dance With Me

Finding Our Spiritual Husband in Christ

❧

*I*n *His Needs, Her Needs,* Willard F. Harley, Jr. identifies from his counseling experience a woman's top five most basic needs in the marriage relationship. In order of importance, they are affection, conversation, honesty and openness, financial support, and family commitment.[1] In this chapter we will discuss affection, conversation, and honesty and openness. Family commitment and financial support will be discussed in chapters eight and ten, respectively.

Women's Needs

I believe these needs are basic to the feminine nature even outside the marriage relationship. They existed before we met our husbands and certainly did not vanish upon their death. They are the unmet needs that drive our loneliness as widows. I believe, though, that God will meet them as the husband He promised to be in Isaiah 54:4–6.

Here Isaiah refers to Israel's history and reveals that the Lord will call and embrace Israel, whom He had forsaken. God compares Israel to a widow who has been "forsaken and grieved in spirit" and reassures her she is not alone because He will be the husband she needs. Isaiah intended this illustration to reassure her of God's faithfulness in difficult circumstances. The widow can claim this promise as well. The Jewish culture was evidently very familiar with God's heart for the widow.

The verses we studied in chapter two reveal how God faithfully attends to the widow. As her creator, God knows the widow's nature and needs do not change when her husband dies. He knows her desires must be tended to and nurtured if her brokenness is to be healed. The question is, "How do we learn to receive nurturing and tenderness from a holy God?" We might not think God is interested in our craving for affection and conversation, but it is His desire and pleasure to engage us at our deepest level.

Once, when my husband was bedfast, a neighbor brought in a meal. She had made some soup for her family and decided to share it with us. She also brought four small cups of tapioca pudding, unaware that I had been wishing for some just days before. Tapioca pudding is one of my favorite desserts. God knew what I had been thinking and made a tender provision for me through our neighbor. Her gesture was the result of an unspoken oneness between God and me. It reminds me of a husband whose smiling eyes lock with his wife's across a crowded room. The intimacy of their relationship allows him to know her thoughts without a word being spoken between them. We can experience this same intimacy with a holy God.

The Scriptures use the analogy of marriage, the most intimate of human bonds, to describe the relationship of Christ to the church. He is her husband. She is His bride. Believing widows, of course, are members of the church, so it is helpful to understand that spiritual relationship. Ray VanderLaan's video series, *Life Lessons Through the Promised Land,*[2] beautifully describes the Jewish tradition of betrothal and its similarity to Christ's commitment to the church until His return.

According to Jewish tradition, when a young woman comes of age she is given an alabaster jar of oil. This jar will be broken at her future husband's feet when a contract for marriage is finalized. At that time the fathers of the future bride and groom seal the contract by sharing a glass of wine. The intended husband returns home with his father, and together they build an addition onto the father's house.

In the meantime, the bride-to-be prepares for the wedding ceremony and awaits the groom's return. She does not know how long it will take the bridegroom to finish the preparations for their new home. She is known in the community as "one who has been redeemed." When the addition to the father's house has been completed, the bridegroom will come to the bride's home with a large wedding party.

After the marriage ceremony, the groom will take his bride into her father's house where the marriage will be immediately consummated. His groomsman will wait at the doorway for the voice of the groom telling him the deed

Chapter 7

has been done. The announcement is made to the guests and seven days of feasting and celebration follow.[3]

Note the parallels in this tradition for us today. Our betrothal to Christ begins at the moment of salvation; we are the brides-to-be of Christ. While He prepares a place for us (John 14), we are to prepare for His return. Part of that preparation involves our surrender to three things: our identity in Christ, His indwelling Spirit, and our daily sanctification. This surrender takes place in part as we experience the trials intended to draw us near to our Lord. Our spiritual union with Christ in eternity will be followed by the marriage supper of the Lamb, and we will be ushered into the mansion that Christ has prepared for us (Revelation 20 and 21). We will spend eternity loving and experiencing God, filled with praise and worship of Him. How awesome!

Affection

God's promises bring security about our eventual union with Him and that enables us to trust Him for our present needs. Dr. Willard Harley regards affection as the number one need of women.[4] The first and hardest loss a widow will experience will not be the sexual relationship but the desire for affection, attention, and the sense of being loved by a man. Studies show that teenage daughters crave their father's affection at an early age. If that father-daughter relationship is not developed, teenage girls may become promiscuous as they seek to fill their need for male affection.

A widow experiences that same need for male companionship. This can become a great struggle, one that

_116_

Satan will use against her. The tendency will be to seek to meet that need prematurely in an inappropriate relationship. We must be sure that our relationship with God is the one that fills and satisfies us first. Only then will we be able to enter into other healthy relationships.

God's love for you is greater than any other love you can experience. If it is affection you crave, He is capable of giving it. You must learn to look for God's affection. As in my illustration of the tapioca pudding, God knows how to extend tenderness to you. He knows what it will take to touch your heart. It will be a personal tenderness that may surprise you, but don't mistake it for an unrelated coincidence. Begin to look for the tenderness and affection of God.

A widowed friend once shared with me that after her husband died, she never felt loneliness at night. When she lay down to sleep, she felt the arms of God holding her. I always thought the scene of the apostle John leaning his head on Jesus' breast at the Last Supper was such a tender picture. When I lay my head on my pillow at night, I try to imagine this scene: I am with God in my room and He is watching over me through the night. I am in His presence. His tender love for me is a sweet and safe place. Psalm 139:17–18 says, "How precious also are your thoughts to me, O God! How vast is the sum of them! If I should count them, they would outnumber the sand. When I awake, I am still with You." Notice that He is not with us, but we are with Him. "For the eyes of the LORD move to and fro throughout the whole earth that He may strongly support those whose heart is completely His" (2 Chron. 16:9).

God wants us to spend time with Him so He can fulfill our need for companionship. You are with Christ wherever you go. Be aware of His presence. Speak out loud to Him. Cry to Him and give up your pain. Laugh with Him when no one else is around. When you feel like you are all alone, remind yourself that you are with Him. Include God in every event, decision, and emotion. Make Him the first one you consult.

Sexual Relationship

Although sexual need is not on Dr. Harley's list, I think it is important to discuss it here. As time passes, you may find yourself struggling with the loss of a sexual relationship. This is a difficult issue that you must ask God to settle for you. As I speak to widows who are willing to share their feelings, I find there are a myriad of ways they try to satisfy this physical desire. Often we are too embarrassed to talk about our feelings or acknowledge even to ourselves that we are struggling. Remember, though, that God is aware of these deep emotions.

If you find yourself desiring a sexual relationship, don't be embarrassed or feel that you have sinned. God has given us a sexual nature. When you struggle with sexual tension, the best solution is to ask God to quiet that tension. When sexual tension reaches a peak, your body may naturally release it through a physical orgasm similar to when you were married. Be honest with God about your physical desires. He already knows when you are struggling.

The danger for us during this vulnerable time is when we dwell on our sexual desires or look to satisfy them on our own. If we do not look to God for help with this struggle, we may find ourselves tempted to enter into a relationship outside of marriage or into an ill-advised marriage. To do so is dangerous because it risks becoming a widow who "gives herself to wanton pleasure" and "is dead while she lives" (I Tim. 5:6).

Be careful, therefore, about what you feed into your mind. Be cautious and discerning about what you watch on TV and at the movies. Think carefully about what you choose to read. What are you listening to on the radio? Remember, "Each one is tempted when he is carried away and enticed by his own lust" (James 1:14). That's why Paul tells Timothy that he wants "younger widows to get married, bear children, keep house... (1 Timothy 5:14)."

I hope I do not offend readers by my frankness on this topic, but these desires are a natural part of our God-created nature. We cannot pretend they don't exist. If we do, Satan will use our denial as a foothold to defeat us at some point along the way. "Finally, brethren, whatever is true, whatever is honorable, whatever is right, whatever is pure, whatever is lovely, whatever is of good repute, if there is any excellence and if anything worthy of praise, dwell on these things" (Philippians 4:8). We must take every thought captive to the obedience of Jesus Christ (2 Cor. 10:5). God will provide for your sexual desires if you ask.

Remarriage may become an option for you. Some widows say they would never marry again because they feel it would be an act of betrayal. If remarriage is God's intention for your life, He will prepare you to accept new direction. It is not disloyal to remarry. In fact, as a widow friend once said to me, "It is one of the greatest compliments we can give to our previous relationship when we desire to enter into a marriage covenant again."

The United States Census Bureau reports that in the year 2000 there were 11.1 million widows in this country.[5] Statistically, nearly ninety percent of all widows will remarry[6] and eighty percent of widows under fifty will remarry within five years.[7] I know widows who have remarried in their 80s! The sexual relationship can be just as important in this season of life as any other. Single believers should not be focused on seeking a mate, but rather on seeking God.

In 1 Corinthians 6 and 7, Paul specifically teaches about the focus and behavior God desires for the single believer, which includes the widow. In this season of life we are instructed to care for the things of the Lord and to strive to be holy in both body and spirit. It is a time when our attention should be focused on our relationship with the Lord in spiritual growth and renewal, not divided to include the things of the world. God will direct you regarding further relationships according to His plan and timing. It may not be His intention for you to be widowed for a long time, or He may desire to use you greatly as a widow. Whatever His plan, know that He will be with you and will give you joy as you follow Him.

Until these choices become clear, we must refocus the lost physical relationship with our husbands on a stronger, exclusive oneness in Christ. That oneness with the Lord is what God intended the physical union to symbolize in the first place. We need to commit ourselves to spending time and energy developing this oneness. Christ was praying for this when He prayed in the Garden of Gethsemane before His crucifixion:

> I do not ask on behalf of these [the disciples] alone but for those also who believe in Me through their word; that they may all be one… that the world may believe that You sent Me. The glory which You have given Me I have given to them, that they may be one, just as We are one; I in them and You in Me, that they may be perfected in unity, so that the world may know that You sent Me, and loved them, as You have loved Me (John 17:20–23).

Conversation

Don't ever apologize for spending time in the Word, listening to the voice of your husband, God, as He draws your heart to Himself. Meditating on God's Word requires time set aside from our daily schedule. We don't think it is wasted time when we spend hours in conversation on the phone or with friends with whom we are developing relationships. We must spend time on any relationship to bring it to the level of companionship. We should do no less with Christ. If you have a hectic schedule, sit down and evaluate your activity.

Satan will try to keep you from quiet times with the Lord. Sometimes we go to God's Word only to do an assignment or perform an obligated "quiet time" once a day. We fit God into our schedule as it is convenient for us. Once we have met our obligation, though, how often do we spontaneously return to God's Word for further encounter with Him? If we desire Christ to be our husband and companion, we will need to re-examine our behavior. It can't be much of a relationship if the time spent with our husband is forced into a once-a-day obligation.

I found it helpful to wait on Christ to call me to His Word. I gleaned this idea from Jeremiah 29:11–14a.

> For I know the thoughts that I think toward you, saith the LORD, thoughts of peace, and not of evil, to give you an expected end. Then shall ye call upon me, and ye shall go and pray unto me, and I will hearken unto you. And ye shall seek me, and find me, when ye shall search for me with all your heart. And I will be found of you, saith the LORD (KJV).

This passage describes an interactive relationship. So, when the Lord prompts me to read my Bible, I consider it a priority—as if my husband had just called me on the phone and said, "Hey, let's meet for lunch. Can you get away?" God knows what's going on in your life. He will call you accordingly.

My determination to respond to God's promptings was the beginning of Christ's wooing me. I would become so excited to think that He was asking me to spend time with Him. I felt so loved and special. Now when I go to the Word, there always seems to be something specific He is calling me to consider. I use my concordance and dictionary to look up verses and word meanings and cross-reference verses in my Bible. I may look at several translations as I study. Sometimes I read without deep study and merely listen to what God is teaching me as I meditate and consider His truths. I often interact with Him concerning the verses I am reading as I pray through them. Most of the time I read the Scriptures out loud to keep my mind focused. At other times I will take a walk and listen to portions of the Bible on tape. These unique spiritual experiences are the best part of my day. Don't be afraid to talk with God out loud—in your car or the privacy of your home. Interact with Him as the living, omnipresent God.

I eventually came to the point where it seemed I was always thinking about the Lord. I began to be in a constant attitude of prayer in my daily activities. I conversed with Him, bared my soul to Him, and felt that He listened compassionately to what concerned me. Always stretching me to look deeper into my heart, He revealed my sin and exposed the lies that had given the enemy a foothold in my life. He opened every door and cleaned every closet of His temple.

Honesty

He had been my Savior and sovereign God all along, but now I felt Him becoming my husband and desired companion. I was falling in love with Him. For the first time in my spiritual walk I was beginning to know the Lord intimately and loving Him more every day. And you know what? I wasn't lonely any more. Not that I didn't miss my earthly husband or think about him with tender affection, but the memories no longer brought sharp pain. The recollections had been softened by the tenderness of Christ in my life. My relationship with the Lord had become one of fulfillment and honesty.

My husband used to send me flowers every year on our anniversary. He was in the Air National Guard and was required to go to some remote place for a two-week summer duty every year. Without exception, his two weeks on duty separated us on our special date. I am very big on dates, and celebrating things *on the exact date* is very important to me! His way of making up for not being with me was to send flowers. I loved it! In the years following his death I really missed those tender moments. One year in particular I had been pining about it, and a few months later my sister surprised me by sending a dozen yellow roses for my birthday. I knew as soon as I opened the box that God was using her to fulfill the longing of my heart for this very tender moment.

The tender affections of God toward us are His response to the conversation, honesty, and openness we share with Him. Remember, one of our top five basic needs as women is honesty and openness. Do you allow yourself to be completely broken and exposed before God? He desires that from you. Study these verses to discover the importance of openness and honesty before the Lord as He enters into dialogue with us: Psalm 14:2; 51:10–13, 16–17; 73:25–28; 116:1–2; 121.

Conversation, honesty, and openness with the Lord cannot occur until we are willing to remove all boundaries. It begins with a full confession of our sin. It requires worship in our most private time with Christ. That worship may involve weighing our thoughts against His Word, responsive prayer to that meditation, confession, singing, praise, playing instruments, and dancing.

Enjoy God

Perhaps this sounds strange to more conservative readers, but the Scriptures often speak of dancing before the Lord. In most cases, dancing is practiced in combination with singing and praise to God. The children of Israel danced before the Lord after victories in battle. When David brought the ark of God back to the city after defeating the Philistines, he danced before the Lord with all his might (2 Samuel 6:14). There was much dancing and celebration after the death of Sisera and Jabin, enemies of God's people (Judges 4:21–5:1). After God helped Israel subdue these enemies, the words to Deborah and Barak's victory song fill chapter five. After the children of Israel crossed the Red Sea, they sang to the Lord (Exodus 15:1–18), and Miriam the prophetess took a timbrel in her hand and led the women in a dancing celebration (v. 20). God's people danced in celebration of battle victories, in times of worship and praise, and just from the pure joy of having the Lord in their lives.

So many times we go to church and sing beautiful songs of worship that invite the Lord's presence. We sing about our desire to dance with Him, yet we stand erect and motionless, afraid we might lose control. Do you ever dance with the Lord? Dancing with the Lord and lifting up your hands to Him in worship and praise can be a very special moment in the privacy of your quiet time. Speak Him into your presence, invite Him to be spiritually intimate with you, and let the music and His Spirit indwell you. This all requires an openness and honesty before the Lord. Don't limit His response. Don't accept a God that is too small.

Enjoy God! Love Him with all your heart, with all your soul, with all your mind, and with all your strength. He will release your lonely brokenness. He will call you to Himself in a place reserved for you alone—a healing place that you will never want to leave.

Study Guide
Chapter 7: Dance with Me
(See page vi for instructions for using the study guide.)

1. What Bible truths can you identify in this chapter as precious promises from Christ that relate to affection, intimacy, conversation, and honesty and openness?

2. What key verses will you add to your key ring?

3. Perhaps you have never considered what an intimate relationship with God, from His perspective, would look and feel like. As you come to God in prayer, spend time in quietness and meditation without expectation— just be in His presence and wait for Him to engage you. Begin by thinking of God as the companion you have lost in your husband. What steps will you take to see

yourself as God sees you and respond freely to His desire to love and nurture you? What changes will you make so that you can develop a personal relationship with Him? These steps must replace the habits you have had in the past.

4. In addition to your regular routine of prayer and study in the Word this week, ask God to interact with you spontaneously. As you go through your day, think of the times your mind turns to God as a personal invitation to spend time with Him. You may respond to His invitation by encountering Him in His Word, putting on some music that draws the meditation of your heart to Him, worshiping Him in dance, journaling your thoughts, or whatever you may feel led to do. Make your interactions with Him a chorus of events throughout the day in addition to your constant mind of prayer. It may feel odd at first, but once you make this your habit, it will become a natural and welcomed part of your life. You will experience the companionship of the Lord as a husband to the widow in the way He intended.

5. If you practice these principles, you will receive fulfillment and deliverance from loneliness. Every widow has these companionship struggles. If you deny that they exist or try to replace them with busyness, you will miss out on the beautiful blessing of deep relationship. List the areas of loneliness you are now experiencing and give them to the Lord. Ask Him to show you how He desires to be your companion with each one.

If we are to have openness and honesty in any relationship, there first must be trust. We have to believe that the other person is who she presents herself to be. It is no different in our relationship with Christ. There is a great difference between believing in God and believing Him, though it may sound the same on the surface. God has given us some very specific directives on how to love Him.

A specific study on Loving God can be accessed at **www.widowtowidow.net** in Chapter Four under the Study Guide Tab. Other studies related to this chapter can be accessed in Chapter Seven under the Study Guide Tab on subjects such as:

• Believing God vs. Believing in God.

Chapter 8

Presence Of The Invisible
The Unseen Father of Our Children

❧

As mothers struggling to help hurting children cope with the loss of their father, widows often find themselves without support from extended family or church members. Since many have not experienced a loss of that kind, they don't know how to help. Your children's struggles will be similar to yours, but they may not cope as well, depending partly on their age. We all grieve and practice our faith in different ways, so our children's responses will likely be as varied as their personalities.

Children's Struggle with Death

This may be your children's first experience with death, and they will have to wrestle with the reality that relationships cannot be taken for granted. The safety that home and family have always provided has been violated, and they may feel the world is spinning out of control. Their reactions will be controlled by their fears, their confusion about life's meaning, and their doubts about God.

To regain control, they may feel an urgent need to redefine their world. They will test every relationship and every other constant, and they may be brutal in their evaluations. On some level, even loved ones they have always trusted will become the enemy in their minds. It is best to give them as many choices as you can. They desperately need answers that you may not have because discovering life anew will be your task, as well. This is a faith-walk you will have to take without the advantage of prior experience. Things will never be the same; so don't imagine that someday you will all return to what everyone thinks is "normal."

Navigating these changes through uncharted waters is difficult because the dynamics are different in every family. Remember the continuum from chapter one (from victim to survivor to thriver). Try not to let your children get stuck along the way by creating an identity or choosing a life course from their center of pain. Hold the line from the God you know to be true.

Although your children may challenge all you have taught them, be faithful to trust the Lord. In time, they will realize that truth and God's promises do not change. Take one day at a time and keep the communication lines open. You will have to let God lead you as you assure your children it is okay to move on. Imagine they are hooked to a rubber band that is being stretched. They may be pulled away from you temporarily, but eventually the band will reach its limit, and they will return. God is the balance, so center yourself in Him.

Teenagers who lose a parent to death react in predictable patterns. Unlike their peers, who tend to feel a sense of immortality, these teenagers will be haunted by the reality that life can be short and unpredictable. Out of that helplessness they may attempt to live life with as much gusto as possible before theirs is taken also. They may want to marry young and start their families early. Often their efforts to establish career patterns will be less conventional, taking risky shortcuts along the way. A traditional four-year college pathway may seem lengthy and undesirable to them. They may demonstrate an aggressive urgency to take control of their lives instead of trusting the Lord. We should encourage them to lean wholly on the Lord, but it may be a solution they are unwilling to accept. These are painful scenes to witness, and our only hope is to entrust our children to Christ.

Some of you may still be raising younger children at home; others may have adult children. No matter what your circumstances, it is hard to know how to capture God's vision for your children. You may find yourself asking how their father would have handled this problem. Often we try to be both father and mother to our hurting children or seek some kind of substitute father through extended family, friends, or the church. I believe God wants us to claim His promise that He will be the father to the fatherless. Don't make substitutions for God; just trust Him with your whole heart. It will require a lot of time on your knees, but God will provide the answer. He will guide you through if you will wait on Him.

We learned earlier that in the Old Testament the husband's brother was responsible for carrying on the family name and bearing children for the lost husband. I think Paul alludes to this tradition when he says to Timothy, "But if any widow have children or nephews, let them learn first to shew piety at home, and to requite their parents: for that is good and acceptable before God" (1 Timothy 5:4, KJV). The children have been commanded to requite, or as the NASB phrases it, "to make some return." That does not mean, however, that the son is to be a substitute for the father. God has promised to be a husband to the widow, so that role is filled. Don't be tempted, therefore, to become co-dependent in your relationship with your son. It is so easy to do, but Satan will use it to defeat you later.

Guidelines for Raising Children

God's Word provides sound guidelines for raising children. At times you may seek godly counsel from those you feel are wise and have control over their household, but always measure their advice prayerfully against the standard of God's Word. Everyone will have advice, so be cautious about unsolicited ideas. If you make mistakes—and you will—God will work them for good (Rom. 8:28). Let me share some general thoughts on child rearing that I think might be helpful.

Proverbs 22:6, "Train up a child in the way he should go: and when he is old, he will not depart from it" (KJV). I have observed that this verse often becomes a discouraging snare to parents instead of the promise God intended it to be. There are two parts to the verse. First is the command to train up a child in the way he should go, and second is the promise that when the child is old, he will not depart from the way he should go. Confusion about the meaning of this verse is widespread. It does not say that if we do well in training our children, they will not depart from God, nor does it say if we don't do a good job, they will depart. If this were true, God would be eliminated from the formula, because the success would be dependent on the work we performed, not on Him.

Our Part

The command is to train up a child in the way he should go. That is clearly our part as parents as we are empowered by God. We accomplish that in a myriad of ways. Deuteronomy 6:4–25 is a powerful source of wisdom concerning God's design for parents. The passage teaches us that we train by our words, testimony, and observed actions. Our actions observed by our children are the most powerful training tool. The saying, "Actions speak louder than words," definitely applies here. Sadly, however, sometimes our lives more clearly say, "Do as I say, not as I do." Remember, God is the unseen party acting to work in the child's heart through our testimony. We will make mistakes, but we must entrust the children to God. He has promised a special grace and faithfulness to our fatherless children.

To have victory in our training, we must follow Deuteronomy 6:4–5, recognizing the one true God and committing personally to love Him with all our heart, soul, and might. "And thou shalt teach them [the words of God] diligently unto thy children, and shalt talk of them when thou sittest in thine house, and when thou walkest by the way, and when thou liest down, and when thou risest up" (Deuteronomy 6:7, KJV). The Word of God should so extend into your heart that it saturates your daily conversations.

You do not have to quote Scripture to your children constantly, but if the Word is in your heart, it will control the wisdom that comes out of your mouth. "For the mouth speaks out of that which fills the heart. The good man brings out of his good treasure what is good; and the evil man brings out of his evil treasure what is evil" (Matt. 12:34b–35). The words of God are to be on our hearts so they can come from the inside out—otherwise we are just making noise.

Furthermore, the Word of God, which is in our heart, will be observed by our children when they see us. "…[B]ind them for a sign upon thine hand, and they shall be as frontlets between thine eyes" (Deuteronomy 6:8, KJV). When our children see us making daily decisions based on our trust in God, they see His influence as if it were bound as a sign upon our hand. They see that our vision for the future comes from God. They see our dependence on the Lord and that we pray over every decision. They learn that we wait for the Lord's answers to the difficult issues we face as a family. The trust we have in the Lord is a strong tower before them. They see the invisible through His visible provisions as we give Him credit for them. Our anchor in the Lord will become theirs.

We teach the Word of God to our children when we adorn our home with it. "And you shall write them on the doorposts of your house, and on your gates" (Deuteronomy 6:9). Are our homes splashed with biblical truth? Do we have pictures with Bible verses on the walls? Are there verses from God's Word taped to our mirrors and refrigerators as a memorization tool? Can the Word of God be observed on our doorposts and gates? This is where godly women can use their talents and gifts to decorate. Do you realize that the Lord Himself has something to say about how you decorate your home? It is here in this haven that our children will learn to revere and fear the Lord. It is here they will learn who He is.

When our children go out into the world, they will compare it with their home experiences. The difference must be striking! If our homes are not different from the ways of the world, our children will not be well equipped to stand against the enemy who is lurking on the other side of the door. Know that the enemy desires to come home with them at night.

When the children of Israel went into the rich land God had promised them, they found it filled with idolatry. God warned them in Deuteronomy 6:12–13, "Watch yourself, that you do not forget the LORD who brought you from the land of Egypt…You shall fear only the LORD your God; and you shall worship Him and swear by His name." To fear God is to respect and revere His authority. Why is the fear of the LORD so important in our lives? It is the fear of the LORD that causes men to depart from evil (Prov. 16:6). Just as God trained the children of Israel to fear Him in the wilderness, so we must train our children to the same end.

God told Israel that they were not to "...follow other gods, any of the gods of the peoples who surround you" (Deuteronomy 6:14). That directive applies to our children too as they daily enter the world outside their home.

When your children's peers are in bondage to the gods of pornography, sexual lust, drug addiction, alcoholism, love of money, or eating disorders, Satan will tempt *them* to desire those gods as well. Training our children in the way they should go requires us to expose these behaviors as idolatry and clearly explain why. Our children's choice to trust God and not the idols of their culture will be evidence of the faith *they* choose.

Sadly, the same behaviors you warn your children about are practiced in some of our Christian homes and churches. We need to evaluate carefully where our family places its trust. Remind your children God is a jealous God (Deuteronomy 6:15), and we are to "...diligently keep the commandments of the LORD [our] God, and His testimonies, and His statutes which he has commanded [us]" (Deuteronomy 6:17). As we include our children in these evaluations, we invite everyone to be involved in guarding the gate of our home.

When we diligently and sensitively pursue biblical training in our homes, God can use it to accomplish His promise in the second part of Proverbs 22:6, "...when he is old he will not depart from it." Our part is a command; God's part is a promise.

I have two children who were "trained up in the way they should go" by two Christian parents. When my husband died, everything we had ever taught them suddenly came into question. Did that negate the years of training that preceded? No. Did their stumbling and failure mean the training wasn't what it should have been? No. Did my husband and I fail to do the job? No. Did we make mistakes along the way? Of course! But it is not the quality of our training that guarantees a child will walk with Christ. That is God's work.

God's Part

The second part of the verse does not begin until the first is complete. The first part involves our effort to train as directed and empowered by God, but the second part has a little twist. We must get out of God's way and let Him complete the work He began through us. We must not let Satan defeat us through fear and our attempts to take control, as we witness what God is doing in the lives of our older children. As awful as it may look, let's not panic when the prodigal son leaves! We have to release him—God is going with him. We must be sure to communicate that we love him and will always be there for him. Let's get on our knees because that is our role in the second season. I believe God gave me children so I could learn to pray. I remember Peter's words:

> Beloved, do not be surprised at the fiery ordeal among you, which comes upon you for your testing, as though some strange thing were happening to you; but to the degree that you share the sufferings of Christ, keep on rejoicing, so that also at the revelation of His glory you may rejoice with exultation (1 Peter 4:12, 13).

> In this you greatly rejoice, even though now
> for a little while, if necessary, you have been
> distressed by various trials, so that the proof
> of your faith, being more precious than gold
> which is perishable, even though tested by
> fire, may be found to result in praise and glory
> and honor at the revelation of Jesus Christ
> …obtaining as the outcome of your faith the
> salvation of your souls (1 Peter 1:6–7, 9).

These are the great and precious promises of God for our children and us! If we accept trials for the proving of our own faith, why do we feel that we have failed as parents when our children go through the same process for the proving of theirs? Joshua said, "Now, therefore, fear the LORD, [there is that fear of the LORD again] and serve Him in sincerity and truth…If it is disagreeable in your sight to serve the LORD, choose for yourselves today whom you will serve…but as for me and my house, we will serve the LORD" (Joshua 24:14–15).

Joshua chose for his household to serve the Lord. We do the same with our children from the time they are born, but at some point during their teenage years, they will also have to choose for themselves. Later, they will have to choose for their own household. We hope the choice for Christ will be immediate and without hesitation. It seems, however, that for some it is not, regardless of how they were trained. For them the decision to follow Christ may not come until after they have tried every other option. They were the children who were always edging their toe across the line just to be sure that the line was still where you said it was—always testing. Be assured that God will use all this—the good, the bad, and the ugly. And it may get very ugly before it is over. Do not blame yourself for the choices your children make. You cannot control them at this point, nor does God intend for you to do so. Don't measure your self-worth by their behavior. Your identity is in Christ alone, not in your role as a parent.

I think the hardest part for parents is the transition from the command to train (Proverbs 22:6) to the promise God says He will perform in our children's lives. Resistance and sometimes rebellion precede our prodigal children's decision for Christ. A lot depends on the strength and will that God has set into the nature of the child, but remember that in it all God is in control.

As I struggled with the pain of what I thought was failure in training my own prodigal children, a friend sent me a helpful e-mail. For those who parent as Christ-followers, it illustrates the difference between God's command for us to train and His promise to finish the work He has begun in our children's lives. I was feeling discouraged and blamed myself for teenage children who did not immediately choose to follow Christ. This e-mail changed my thinking, and I include it here for your consideration.

> A man was sleeping at night in his cabin when suddenly his room was filled with light, and God appeared. The Lord told the man he had work for him to do, and showed him a large rock in front of his cabin. The Lord

explained that the man was to push against the rock with all his might. So, this the man did, day after day. For many years he toiled from sun up to sun down; his shoulders set squarely against the cold, massive surface of the unmoving rock, pushing with all of his might. Each night the man returned to his cabin sore and worn out, feeling that his whole day had been spent in vain. Since the man was showing discouragement, the Adversary (Satan) decided to enter the picture by placing thoughts into the weary mind: "You have been pushing against that rock for a long time, and it hasn't moved," thus, giving the man the impression that the task was impossible and that he was nothing but a failure.

These thoughts discouraged and disheartened the man. *Why kill myself over this?* he thought. *I'll just put in the rest of my time, giving just the minimum effort; and that will be good enough.* And that is what he planned to do, until one day he decided to make it a matter of prayer and take his troubled thoughts to the Lord.

"Lord," he said, "I have labored long and hard in your service, putting all my strength to do that which you have asked. Yet, after all this time, I have not even budged that rock by half a millimeter. What is wrong? Why am I failing?" The Lord responded compassionately, "My friend, when I asked you to serve Me and you accepted, I told you that your task was to push against the rock with all of your strength, which you have done. Never once did I mention to you that I expected you to move it. Your task was to push. And now you come to Me with your strength spent, thinking that you have failed. But, is that really so? Look at yourself. Your arms are strong and muscled, your back sinewy and brown, your hands are callused from constant pressure, your legs have become massive and hard. Through opposition you have grown much, and your abilities now surpass that which you used to have. Yet you haven't moved the rock. But your calling was to be obedient and to push and to exercise your faith and trust in My wisdom. This you have done. Now I, My friend, will move the rock."

At times, when we hear a word from God, we tend to use our own intellect to decipher what He wants, when actually what God wants is just a simple obedience and faith in Him. By all means, exercise the faith that moves mountains, but know that it is still God who moves them.[1]

God has a plan for each of our children. He knows just what preparations are required to equip them for that plan. He is looking at the big picture. We parents are looking with human eyes at just a small piece. Don't get in the way of His preparation by sheltering your children from failure. Allow them the freedom to question God. When God calls them, He wants total commitment. He does not want our children to be looking over their shoulders, wondering if the world might have better answers. They must be solid in their decision for Him. If a prodigal trip is necessary for your child, trust God through it. He has promised to be a father to the fatherless. He will make the trip with them.

In speaking of Christ on the cross, Isaiah writes, "…the LORD was pleased to crush Him, putting him to grief…As a result of the anguish of His soul, He will see it and be satisfied" (Isaiah 53:10, 11). If God the Father would allow His own Son to be crushed for our sin and iniquity, as the Father to the fatherless he will surely not spare our prodigal children from suffering. Christ was crushed and utterly forsaken on the cross by His own Father for the very sins our prodigal children commit. The same power that raised Christ from the dead is at God's disposal to deliver our children from their sin and love of the world, bringing them to a faith relationship, surrendered to Him for eternity.

We must not fear that they will be forsaken, because Christ can see their hearts and discern what is too much for them to endure. We must pray for the courage to step back and let God have His way with them. "No temptation has overtaken you but such as is common to man; and God is faithful, who will not allow you to be tempted beyond what you are able, but with the temptation will provide the way of escape also, that you may be able to endure it" (1 Corinthians 10:13). The way of escape is always in full surrender to Christ.

Remember Abraham? He was the man who believed God, and it was counted as righteousness (see Genesis 15:6). God promised Abraham He would give the land he lived in to his descendants—as far as the eye could see north, south, east, and west. But for Abraham's entire life the land was inhabited by other nations. He even had to purchase a place to bury his wife. God also promised Abraham his descendants would be as numerous as the stars, but when he died he had only two heirs of the promise. Hundreds of years later, when the children of Israel entered the Promised Land, his descendants were as numerous as the stars (see Genesis 15).

Are you walking by faith or sight when it comes to your children? Trust God for the promise in Proverbs 6:22, and don't worry about whether or not you live to see it. Lift them up in prayer without putting conditions on God. It might seem as though they will never get there, but God will deliver!

If you are a widow who has just found the Lord or one who didn't train up your children as God commanded, start where you are today. If your children are still at home, begin now to train them. If they are past the season to train in your home, let your testimony and trust in the Lord shine before them. Confess to the LORD the times you did not trust Him, and accept His forgiveness (see 1 John 1:9). Don't let Satan defeat you by continually taking you back to your failure because the Lord says, "I, even I, am the one who wipes out your transgressions for My own sake, and I will not remember your sins" (Isaiah 43:25).

Satan will constantly accuse you of sin you have already confessed before the Lord. In *The Christian's Secret of a Happy Life,* Hannah Whitall Smith tells of a woman who was able to find victory with this struggle. When she was brought into condemnation and discouragement by accusations the enemy railed against her, she simply proclaimed, "The Lord is my Helper; take them to Him, and settle them in His presence"—and that was the end of it![2]

The Testimony of Quiet Behavior

One of the most powerful passages in Scripture for Christian women is 1 Peter 3:1–2, "In the same way, you wives, be submissive to your own husbands so that even if any of them are disobedient to the word, they may be won without a word by the behavior of their wives, as they observe your chaste and respectful behavior." And who is the husband to whom our family will see us in subjection? That husband is our "Maker, whose name is the LORD of hosts…[our] Redeemer is the Holy One of Israel, who is called the God of all the earth" (Isaiah 54:5).

The passage in 1 Peter speaks specifically to wives who are married, but I believe the godly character of a widow who trusts in God can have the same effect on unbelieving children. Actions speak louder than words. God uses our testimony when we do not even know anyone is looking. Only He can change hearts and open eyes. Let us live like the widow who "…has fixed her hope on God and continues in entreaties and prayers night and day" (1 Timothy 5:5). In this our children will find victory for the long journey home.

❧

Study Guide
Chapter 8: Presence of the Invisible
(See page vi for instructions for using the study guide.)

1. What are the precious promises you have discovered concerning your children in this chapter?

2. Add those verses that have special meaning for you to your key ring.

3. As you think about this theme and realize that God has a special concern for His fatherless creation, what new insights on God's perspective have encouraged you? List the ways you can minister to your adult (18 and over) prodigal children that respect their right to choose. In what ways have you crossed boundaries with them?

4. What have you identified specifically in the context of this chapter that you personally need to think differently about? Review Deuteronomy 6:4–25. List the ways you can practice each step of the training process with your children who are still at home.

5. Think about and write out the godly expectations (defined in chapter five) that you can reasonably set concerning your adult children or those who may be in a prodigal experience. It is so tempting to allow your adult children to become your main source of companionship or area of worry, and it's even worse to allow your sons to fill the role of their father. Writing our goals down can help us sort out where the boundaries should be for healthy relationships so that everyone can grow spiritually closer to God and be used by Him for His kingdom purposes.

Additional studies can be accessed at **www. widowtowidow.net** in Chapter Eight under the Study Guide Tab on subjects such as:
- Our Role as Mothers (includes biblical examples of mothers in the parenting role and further thoughts on Proverbs 22:6)
- The Prodigal Son (Luke 15:11–32).

Part Four:

Season Of Surrender

❧

Chapter 9

The Idol Mask

Exposing Idols and
Returning Our Hearts to Christ

❧

Defining Idolatry

*P*erhaps you will be surprised to learn that the exposure of subtle idolatrous practices can play an important part in a widow's struggle for recovery. Some might suggest that compared to other places and other times, the sin of idolatry is not an issue in our nation today. While it is true that the idolatrous rituals of Buddhism and Shintoism may not play a large part in our "Christian" culture, we have replaced carved images and pagan shrines with equally harmful attitudes and behaviors. In fact, these less visible practices can be so subtle that we struggle to identify them.

Let's define more specifically what the practice of idolatry involves. Very simply, idolatry substitutes a dependence on something else—anything else—in place of our trust in God. We must go before God and sincerely ask Him to reveal what is in our hearts concerning the issue of trust.

Identifying Idolatry

God wants to expose any idolatry that exists in our heart so He can cleanse us and draw us to Himself. Satan, however, will use everything at his disposal to keep us in bondage to that idolatry. He knows our weaknesses. He observes our need and offers just the right God-substitutes to meet it. Consider loneliness, for example. We may find ourselves struggling with the loss of companionship when our husbands die. Filling that void outside of Christ is idolatry whether we fill it with eating, shopping, reading, or movies. There is nothing wrong with any of these activities in and of themselves, but they can be used for the purpose of filling the void of loneliness that we should be letting Christ fill. The hard reality for many is that God is not enough on a daily basis, and the biblical truth that Christ is sufficient for all circumstances is not our experience. Until we admit our sense of the insufficiency of Christ in our lives, we will not be able to identify and change our own subtle idolatrous practices.

Our Use of Time

Let's examine why we may not be experiencing God's sufficiency. How much of your time does God consume beyond the once-a-day "quiet time"? If you are not interacting with God throughout the day, you need to make some changes. Maybe in the past you felt that spending hours reading the Bible, praying, and worshiping God were part of a daily routine meant for pastors, not the ordinary church members. Perhaps you would consider such a daily routine an unproductive use of your time.

What is the goal of time spent with God, though? Is it to learn Bible facts and to meet your spiritual obligations, or is it to interact with God and dwell in His presence? Is He a companion who is sufficient for every emotional need? Do you go to the Lord first with your problems? Do you achieve real emotional healing and joy from the time you spend with God? When you have a problem, do you call a friend first, or do you open the Word and use it as a source of consultation? Do you go to the refrigerator as you mull over your problem, not because you are hungry but because it helps to be eating while you try to think? Maybe you go to the mall and shop to get your mind off things, because buying something just makes you feel better.

Why is opening God's Word often the last thing we do as we live out our day? I think it's because we do not know how to interact with God through His Word. We just don't consider God's Word relevant for today's problems. Whatever the reason, we need a new understanding of how to engage God's Word and encounter Him in honest interaction.

Let's look at another example. Imagine that you find yourself home alone without plans for the evening and you don't know what to do. You walk around the house wishing for companionship. Friends are all busy with husbands and family, so how will you decide to spend the next several hours? Will you check out for a while in front of the TV or with a book, or will you choose to spend this time with the Lord? Would He be your first thought or your last? When you want to have a good time do you ever think first of an activity you can do with the Lord? Do you ever spend time with the Lord that results in the same contentment as spending time with a friend or engaging in an activity? If spending time with the Lord became a spontaneous, regular routine, the relationship you have with Him right now would be emotionally sufficient.

We all spend our time doing something. Think about the leisure time some of us have spent focused on our children's sports activities. During athletic championships, how many games have you attended in a week? How much money have you spent and how far have you traveled to participate? Activities like these can become our god and the real God becomes a forgotten blur. Do you know a parent and child who have camped out at the fairgrounds for an entire week, sleeping in a stall with their horse because it was fair week? Every waking minute is controlled by the fair schedule, and it becomes the focus of everyone's attention.

On some level these activities drain our finances, our time, and our energy so that we may have nothing left for the Lord. It is a shame that we are so willing to sacrifice precious time on the altar of activity when we are looking for entertainment or emotional satisfaction.

We all recognize the rapid pace of life today. Activity defines us. As adults, we are typically not involved in just one activity but in two or three so that we need help from friends and family just to navigate our schedules. In addition, our vans may be loaded with children in transit to *their* activities. There is certainly no time for quiet, reflective moments. If it's not our children, then it's our personal calendar.

If someone invites you over for fellowship or to help with a problem, is your schedule so full they have to wait a week or two before you have an open time slot? If you are really on call for the Lord, how spontaneous are you? Is being His ambassador your priority? Referring to the last days, the angel Michael says to Daniel, "...even to the time of the end: many shall run to and fro, and knowledge shall be increased" (Daniel 12:4, KJV). Let there be no doubt, Satan can keep you very busy, so you will have little time left to spend with God or to act on His wishes.

Quiet evenings with the Lord may seem pale and unfulfilling in comparison to the busyness of our lives. For many in our culture, this fixation with activity has become the standard by which we measure our own significance and worth. If we think Christ still has priority in our lives, ask what percentage of our church membership attended the last fellowship or prayer event. Maybe you were one who missed it, so you don't know. Was the attendance low because "everyone is just busy"? What are they busy with— the things of the Lord or the things of the world in the name of "family time"? Sadly, the church is often more about how to burn out than how to be built up.

We need to start changing our priorities. There is nothing sinful about shopping at the mall, going to a movie, or eating out in a restaurant—unless that activity is fulfilling an emotional need. For example, we eat to nourish the body when we experience hunger. If you are eating for emotional reasons—loneliness, sadness, boredom, and so forth—you have an idol problem. If you are in debt, you have an idol problem. The satisfaction of your emotional need is greater than your pocketbook can afford.

Our Use of Money

Want to know what your idols are? Take a good look at your checkbook, equity line balance, and credit card ledger; find out what desires are creating your debt. It probably won't be a surprise to you, but I can promise it will make you uncomfortable, especially if you are desperately trying to justify your behaviors. I know this is true because God brought me to my knees over it, and I watch it happening all around me. I see people who can't live within their means on two full-time incomes.

If you think we don't have idol temples in this world, take another look at our grandiose malls. Drive down the street sometime and look at all the restaurants. Consider the number of car lots around town and think about how much debt is incurred in owning or leasing those cars. If you think we don't perform the ancient practice of offering human sacrifice, consider how many unborn children we sacrifice in abortion because they might inconvenience our lifestyle. Please don't be distracted by taking offense at what you might perceive to be judgmental comments on my part. I am not judging; I just want you to think.

Eliminating Idolatry

An Illustration from History

I recall a Bible study I attended that the Lord used to get my attention on this matter. The study touched on an event in the life of Hezekiah, King of Judah. When Hezekiah became king, the children of Israel were practicing idol worship. They worshiped carved stone and wooden images in their homes. Some of the images might have been worn as jewelry or for protection. According to Scripture, there were also elevated locations around the city where the full images were placed for corporate worship. These designated areas were called "high places." The worship experience may have involved the burning of incense and human sacrifice, as well as immoral behavior.

None of the kings before Hezekiah was successful in removing the high places, which seemed to be the last footholds of idolatry. Hezekiah, though, was empowered by God to lead the people to renewal and purity in their relationship with God. They purified themselves before the Lord according to His requirements. The people were driven to destroy the idols in the land, including the "high places." This was clearly the result of God's work in their hearts.

> Now when all this was finished, all Israel who were present went out to the cities of Judah, broke the pillars in pieces, cut down the Asherim, and pulled down the high places and the altars throughout all Judah and Benjamin,

as well as in Ephraim and Manasseh, until
they had destroyed them all. Then all the sons
of Israel returned to their cities, each to his
possession (2 Chronicles 31:1).

He [Hezekiah] trusted in the LORD, the God
of Israel; so that after him was none like him
among all the kings of Judah, nor among those
who were before him (2 Kings 18:5).

God was pleased that this nation desired to make Him the
exclusive God of their hearts. Because of their devotion, God
healed the people and made their provision and protection
His priority.

When I realized the magnitude of what Hezekiah
accomplished, I was challenged. No one before or after
him was able to do what God enabled him to do concerning
the nation's idolatry. That was no small thing! How many
times have you been admonished to examine your life and
identify your own personal idols because God is a jealous
God? I have often been challenged by the question, "What
are the idols of our time?" Identifying the idol is usually
the easy part. Depending on our motives, activities that
include food, money, sex, relationships, drugs, alcohol,
television, and sports could all become idols that we trust
outside of Christ.

The children of Israel began their struggle with idolatry
hundreds of years before the time of Hezekiah. We are not
unlike them. Even when they were in the wilderness on their
way to the Promised Land, they were tempted to build the

image of a golden calf (see Exodus 32). This was at a time when God Himself was in their presence daily. Idolatry is deception at its best. Its hold on our lives will keep us in bondage without our realizing we are being compromised.

What strikes me most about Hezekiah is his ability through God to virtually eliminate idolatry during his twenty-nine year reign as king. I realized during this study that even though I could identify the idols of my own heart, I did not know how to "utterly destroy them all." As I considered each of my idols, I realized that God hates idolatry because when we practice it we are actually worshiping Satan. What a horrible discovery that should be for us! We would never deliberately worship Satan, but he can be exposed in our idols. Satan desires our worship of him. As widows living without spiritual leadership or the sense of protection that our husbands were able to provide, we are vulnerable to the pull of idolatry. Though God has promised to be our husband, Satan challenges that position.

Establishing Priorities

The Bible tells us that when Hezekiah became king, the first thing he did was to open the doors of the house of the LORD and repair them (see 2 Chronicles 29:3). Let's note some appropriate parallels between that temple and our own bodies, which are also called God's dwelling place (1 Corinthians 6:19). What are the broken doors of our temple? I believe these broken doors could represent the inner place of the heart, since the heart is the director of our actions and words. Scripture reveals that the mouth speaks from what fills the heart (see Matthew 12:34). So how do we examine this heart door for needed repairs?

I think the answer lies in Hezekiah's next action. He called the priests and Levites together for the purpose of consecrating themselves (see 2 Chronicles 29:5). This was so they could enter the house of God and carry the idolatrous uncleanness out. Who are the priests that must be consecrated for the work to be done in our hearts? We are. 1 Peter 2:9 says that we "are a chosen race, a royal priesthood…" In our sin and unworthiness before God, how will we consecrate ourselves?

The word "consecrate," according to Strong's Exhaustive Concordance, means "to fill" or "be full."[1] It is Christ who must fill us and it is His work to cleanse us and prepare our hearts. It is His daily sanctification process that sets us apart and makes us holy. We must ask God, "Search me, O God, and know my heart; Try me and know my anxious thoughts; And see if there be any hurtful way in me, and lead me in the everlasting way" (Psalm 139:23, 24).

We must go before the Lord in a broken and humble spirit, seeking honestly to know our sin in an attitude of confession and repentance. We must commit to being filled with the fullness of Christ. Until we are filled with His light, what is hidden cannot be uncovered!

If you feel you are in a dry place where God is not near, perhaps you need to take another look at your activities and priorities. Re-examine the source of your worth and contentment. Honestly look at the priority you allow Christ to have in your life as you deal with your own life issues.

Once they had consecrated themselves, the priests and Levites went into the house of the Lord and were equipped by God to remove the uncleanness. At that time idols actually stood in the sanctuary of God's house. "So the priests went in to the inner part of the house of the LORD, to cleanse it, and every unclean thing which they found in the temple of the LORD, they brought out to the court of the house of the LORD. Then the Levites received it to carry out to the Kidron valley" (2 Chronicles 29:16). Once we give Christ permission to fill us, we can begin to identify the uncleanness of our hearts and prepare to carry it out of our temple. Only God knows what is in our hearts, and only He can prepare us to accept and act on that information.

As I came to these realizations, I was driven to my knees before God. I wanted to destroy completely the "high places" of my heart. I began by making a list of everything I was trusting in for emotional well-being outside of God alone. What was I hiding from view? I needed to be totally honest through this process of soul searching. I was embarrassed and humbled by my list. Satan mocked me with thoughts of shame and guilt, but focusing on the provision of Christ at the cross silenced the sting of his accusations.

Once you have created your list, the second step is to ask God to show you why each of the idols is important to you. In other words, what needs have you allowed it to satisfy? Each idol represents something to you. Therefore, it is not the substance of the idol itself that is important, but rather what it represents that must be uncovered. This element may be a little harder to identify, but remember that God is with you. Listen to Him. Write down what comes to mind as you prayerfully meditate.

Let me share from my experience. One of my obvious idols was food. After much prayer God showed me—and it was a shock to realize this truth—that food had become my companion. I seldom ate because I was hungry. The truth is I ate so often that there was never any danger of being hungry. I ate when I was lonely, when I was bored, when I was happy and needed to share my happiness, when I was sad and needed to talk, and when I needed to sort through something. I didn't have my husband to talk to now, but I had my food and it was very important to me. It gave me a sense of satisfaction and fulfillment. I knew I wasn't the only one with this idol problem, but that didn't make me feel any better about it. In my extended family all activities are centered on food, including what we eat and who is cooking it.

Food is important to our whole society. Even in the church we brag about our great cooks and what delicious potlucks we have. It has become an "If you feed them they will come" mentality. For me, food had become a source of interaction that took God's place, and guess whose image was hiding behind the face of my food? I didn't like this discovery. This idol had to be taken out to the brook Kidron. It was not the food that was offensive to God, but rather what it represented and how I misused it. He wants to be the focus of my trust when I am lonely, bored, happy, or sad. He wants me to come to Him if I have something to work out. He wants to be the first one I think of because He adores me. He desires to complete my life.

Putting Christ First

The last step in this process of identifying and eliminating our trust in idols is to put Christ in the place of every idol we have listed. We have already identified what the idol represents; now we must ask ourselves how Christ can satisfy this need instead. What steps will we take to turn to Him? Writing these steps down will help you monitor your progress. This process is a heart issue and a faith issue. We must trust God.

An easy place to be trapped in this process is thinking we can simply eliminate our idols because we have identified them and established a plan of action. The idols of Israel were physical gods made with hands. The gods of our heart are not. Because they are of the heart, they are connected to our will. Now we see the real problem coming into focus. Remember what Paul said about the struggle we have against our own will? Romans 7:18 exposes our dilemma. "For I know that nothing good dwells in me, that is, in my flesh; for the willing is present in me, but the doing of the good is not."

Though we know what our idols are and that God needs to take their place, we are unable to find victory outside of Christ. The Lord does not want us to be independent of Him in this process. His great and precious promise for this struggle is found in Ezekiel 36. When God speaks of the idolatry that eventually drove the nation of Israel into captivity, He speaks of bringing them back to Himself.

> It is not for your sake, O house of Israel, that
> I am about to act, but for My holy name,
> which you have profaned among the nations,

> where you went…I will sprinkle clean water
> on you, and you will be clean; I will cleanse
> you from all your filthiness and from all your
> idols. Moreover, I will give you a new heart
> and put a new spirit within you; and I will
> remove the heart of stone from your flesh,
> and give you a heart of flesh. And I will
> put My Spirit within you and cause you to
> walk in my statutes, and you will be careful
> to observe My ordinances…you will be My
> people, and I will be your God…I will save
> you from all your uncleanness…I, the LORD,
> have spoken and will do it (Ezekiel 36:22,
> 25–29, 36).

Wow! What a relief that is! It is not we who have to accomplish this impossible task in our hearts; it is God who must and will. This promise is the only answer for our dilemma.

The heart is the gatekeeper of the temple. When we are filled with Christ, He can help us filter all that enters unless we turn the filter off by denying the Spirit's leading. We still possess a choice. Matthew 6:21 says, "For where your treasure is, there will your heart be also." Jesus said that the kingdom of heaven is like a treasure found in a field. When found, you sell all that you have in order to buy it (see Matthew 13:44). Job said his treasure was in the words of God's mouth (Job 23:12). James calls us to strengthen our hearts because the coming of the Lord is near (James 5:8), and Solomon tells us in Proverbs 4:23 to "watch over your heart with all diligence, for from it flow the springs of life."

For me the easy part was identifying the idols and what they represented. To substitute Christ in their place was something I tried to wrestle with and accomplish on my own until I realized that I needed Christ. We cannot dance around this. Christ is the only one who can cleanse us, and outside of a relationship with Him and surrendering to Him, it is impossible to eliminate our trust in idols. When idolatry defeats me, I am able to have victory over it only by claiming God's promise in Ezekiel 36 and leaning on His strength to accomplish the work.

> Now when the unclean spirit goes out of a man, it passes through waterless places, seeking rest, and does not find it. Then it says, "I will return to my house from which I came"; and when it comes, it finds it unoccupied, swept, and put in order. Then it goes, and takes along with it seven other spirits more wicked than itself, and they go in and live there; and the last state of that man becomes worse than the first. That is the way it will also be with this wicked generation (Matthew 12:43–45).

While we know that evil cannot enter the believer against his will, we should take notice that these idols will be hard to shake permanently. It is something you must be aware of every day as you live in the strength of the Lord. You must always guard your heart so you can keep a close relationship with Him. Remember that with Christ all things are possible.

Because you have first consecrated yourself to God and your daily sanctification is promised, your temple will not be found swept and empty, but filled with the presence of Almighty God. Commit yourself to come to the Lord in humility, confession, and brokenness as you determine to allow Him to remove these idols and your worship of them. Now that the idols have been exposed and you find Satan's face hiding behind them, they should no longer serve a purpose in your life other than to bring disgust and offense to your spirit.

Once Hezekiah and the Levites had identified and taken the uncleanness from the house of the Lord, he and the rulers of the city went there in the presence of the congregation and offered acceptable sacrifice unto God for reconciliation. Our sacrificial lamb is Christ, who is a worthy and acceptable sacrifice for the uncleanness in our hearts.

Don't be so devastated by what you see in yourself that you stop short of the victory. Satan will try to render you helpless by accusing you of your wickedness outside of Christ. Our bold confidence, however, is the public display God made of Christ as our "propitiation in his blood through faith" (Romans 3:25). I love the word "propitiation." It can be defined as "to cover, or hide from view; to blot out." "The sacrifices of God are a broken spirit; a broken and a contrite heart, O God, Thou wilt not despise" (Ps. 51:17).

Hezekiah's victory came directly from God's pleasure as He saw Judah's desire to know and worship Him. As a direct result of this newfound relationship with God, the people were literally driven in mob style to destroy the "high places."

God was now on the throne of their hearts and reigning with full power and authority in their lives.

Here is where my respect for Hezekiah and his leadership grows greatest. How did they set their idols down, walk away from them, and leave them untouched for his entire reign as king? It had to be because they found something more satisfying. That something else was God.

A beautiful story of how God's people rediscovered who He was is told in 2 Chronicles 29:3 through 31:21. It is the story of a nation falling in love with their God so they couldn't help but worship Him with a full heart. They sacrificed to Him, they confessed to Him, and they worshiped and praised Him. "And their voice was heard, and their prayer came to His holy dwelling place, to heaven" (2 Chronicles 30:27).

Hezekiah was focused on getting back to the basics of the Word of God and discovering what spoke to the heart of God. He worshiped God as God desired. "And every work which he began in the service of the house of God in law and in commandment, seeking his God, he did with all his heart and prospered" (2 Chronicles 31:21).

I can assure you that once God had accomplished this great work through Hezekiah, Satan was not happy. I can imagine the sound of his gnashing teeth. He was immediately on the prowl—so he is with us. He will not take our commitment to change lying down, so be on your guard until your habit of going to the Lord becomes automatic.

It is interesting to observe the fruit of this idol destruction in the hearts of the people of Judah. They immediately went to their brothers in the northern tribes of Israel to convince them to commit to the same effort. They were excited to share their rekindled love relationship with God. Some of the tribes responded with change, but the majority hardened their hearts. According to 2 Chronicles 30:10, the people of Judah were mocked by their brothers.

Israel's reaction to Judah is a good example of the kind of behavior we talked about in chapter 1. Even brothers and sisters in Christ may want us to stay as we were. It is more convenient and comfortable for them if our attitudes remain unchanged. As you make changes regarding your own idolatry, there will be those who will mock you. They will accuse you of being too religious. When you draw away from a fixation on activity, it will make them uncomfortable. It will be hard to leave behaviors that were a part of your comfort zone and theirs. You may even lose friends in the process.

The northern tribes of Israel wanted no part of this new idea, and the people of Judah undoubtedly were saddened by their brethren's response. Thankfully their renewed relationship with the Lord was more important to them than their desire for Israel to join them in the change.

We read about how the enemy's attack comes against those who chose to believe and obey the Lord in 2 Chronicles 32:1. "After these acts of faithfulness Sennacherib king of Assyria came and invaded Judah and besieged the fortified cities, and thought to break into them for himself." There will surely be a King Sennacherib at your doorstep when you commit to destroying the idols in your life. Hezekiah's important response to the frightened people of his kingdom should speak to us also.

"Be strong and courageous, do not fear or be dismayed because of the king of Assyria, nor because of all the multitude which is with him; for the one with us is greater than the one with him. With him is only an arm of flesh, but with us is the LORD our God to help us and to fight our battles." And the people relied on the words of Hezekiah king of Judah (2 Chronicles 32:7–8).

As this nation leaned on the God of all sufficiency, He was faithful. He will be faithful to deliver you, as well.

Removing the hidden idols from your heart will require the same steps God directed Hezekiah to take with Judah. Keeping the idols from finding their way back will be God's work in your heart only as you give Him permission to reign. That is an act of your will. You must build a relationship with Christ that is more satisfying than any idol. It will be resisted by the enemy, and your faith will be tested as was Hezekiah's. But I challenge you to "stand fast therefore in the liberty wherewith Christ hath made us free, and be not entangled again with the yoke of bondage" (Galatians 5:1, KJV).

Study Guide
Chapter 9: The Idol Mask
(See page vi for instructions for using the study guide.)

1. What Bible truths have you identified as precious promises from Christ for you to believe and act on that relate specifically to the practice of idolatry?

2. As you continue to add verses to your key ring, be sure to include some that make special note of the practice of idolatry.

3. Take this time now to go before the Lord. As He searches your inner heart, make a list of everything that comes to mind. List anything in your life that you trust or gain emotional peace and reassurance from outside of God alone.

4. As you look over your list, ask God to show you why each of the idols is important to you. What is the need that gives them power? In other words, what does the idol represent?

5. The third step in this process of ending these idolatrous practices is to substitute Christ for every idol we have listed. How can Christ satisfy those needs instead?

It is critical to understand that no matter how much we want to end our idolatry, we are no different from the children of Israel. The removal of these idols from our heart is the exclusive work of God and His grace. He is the only one who can do it. Our work is to make our deep relationship with Him a priority. We must understand how to love Him and how to receive His love as defined by His perspective not ours.

Additional studies can be accessed at **www. widowtowidow.net** in Chapter Nine under the Study Guide Tab, "Idolatry."

Chapter 10

Seven Principles of GOIA
Releasing Financial Control to God

⌘

*O*ur pastor presented a lesson to our congregation that totally changed my attitude about financial matters. In fact, it changed the way I look at everything in my life. I have asked his permission to share a portion of that presentation with you as we discuss this topic of how to manage our finances and related resources as widows.[1] His lesson was basically an explanation of the seven GOIA principles of Scripture. GOIA is an acronym for God Owns It All.

Seven Principles of GOIA

1. God Owns It All.
2. I manage money for God.
3. Every spending decision is a spiritual act.
4. Contentment rules our hearts.
5. Debt is dangerous. Get rid of it. Stay away from it. Use it very, very sparingly.

6. Saving and investing are wise, but we should not put our trust in them.
7. Giving is a gift to the giver.

Principle 1: God Owns It All

On some level every believer is consciously aware that God, as creator, is in total control of His creation. We might not think of that ownership, however, as including our money, homes, clothes, and cars. In Romans 8:32 Paul writes, "He who did not spare His own Son, but delivered Him over for us all, how will He not also with Him *freely give us all things?"* (emphasis added). If God has promised to give us all things, they must first be His to give. The seven principles of GOIA operate on that premise.

We are the storehouses of God's wealth. He lends us His houses to live in until He needs them for another purpose. When we are gone, He will give them to someone else. He gives each one of us an income. He allows us to borrow the cars we drive since we paid for them with the money He gave us. He provides the money for our food and clothes, and as amazing as it may seem at times, He may provide our food and clothes without giving us the money first! He is so free and automatic with His giving that sometimes we forget who is the giver and who is the receiver, especially when it comes to generously giving back a portion to Him. We may even begin to make decisions about the things He has given us as if He no longer has ownership of them.

When my daughter was a little girl, she talked about how much she wanted to be a store cashier. She was fascinated when we went shopping. One day I asked her why she had such a desire to be a cashier and she replied simply, "Just look at how much money they have in their drawer!" When we explained to her that the money in the drawer was not the cashier's to keep but only to manage for the store, she was incredulous.

Principle 2: We Are God's Managers

That brings us to the second principle of GOIA. We are nothing more than managers of God's money—and everything He chooses to give us. If you were the store cashier my daughter longed to be, you would be watched very closely because of the money in your drawer. You would have to give a daily account for it during your shift, and your drawer would have to balance at the end of the day. Making decisions with it outside of already prescribed rules would not be tolerated. If you had questions about its appropriate use, you would have to ask, not assume what the course of action should be. As managers of God's money and gifts we should do no differently. If God were to call for an accounting of your management of His resources and money right now, how would you fare?

Principle 3: Spending, a Spiritual Act

The third principle of GOIA is that every spending decision is a spiritual act. Every decision we make with our money and resources should be considered only after consultation with the owner, God. I believe that God seriously desires to be consulted about how we spend His money and resources. Let me be very clear about what that might look like in practical application. In every decision we make about spending money and acquiring possessions, we must not act without clear leading from the Lord. I believe God wants to interact with us on every decision, even a trip to the grocery store. If we are spending His money, He wants to have input.

Do you pray before you make your grocery list? How about when you balance your checkbook? Do you ask for His direction and discernment so you will not make a mathematical mistake? Are you allowing Him to direct your thinking about purchases for your home? How about your car? What about when you walk into the mall to shop with nothing specific in mind? Are you a compulsive spender or do you plan to spend God's money according to His direction? Ask yourself before you make any purchase, *"Is this a need or only a want? Has God given me clear direction for this purchase or decision?"*

We must put everything we have learned about God and His desire for our lives into practice. We must follow the rules He has given us from His Word. If we are doing that, we will produce the fruit of discipline and obedience. As we manage faithfully, He will give us more responsibility. God wants faithful saints at every socio-economic level. If everyone were in the same class economically, who would relate and give testimony to the others? Our economic status is not a punishment from God. It is not how much money and how many possessions we have that is important to God but how we manage what we do have. If you manage what you have with prayer and by seeking Him, He will bless you with what you need and give you contentment, too.

Principle 4: Contentment Rules Our Hearts

Contentment and its rule in our hearts is the fourth GOIA principle. That contentment will be determined by where our treasure is. If our treasure is in our relationship and identity in Christ, we will be content in any circumstance. Remember that God is jealous for our worship. If our *stuff* takes us away from Him, we are in heart trouble. This takes us back to the issues of idolatry in chapter nine. Prayerfully ask God to reveal the truth of your heart concerning this matter. Allow yourself to be humbled before Him. We could not be content if we did not have what we need from God. If we feel we are lacking, He has told us to ask. Notice that I said, "need," not "desire." He promises in 1 John 5:14–15, " If we ask anything according to His will, He hears us: And if we know that He hears us in whatever we ask, we know that we have the requests which we have asked from Him."

Please consider this truth.

> For everyone who asks receives, and he who seeks finds, and to him who knocks it will be opened. Or what man is there among you, who when his son asks for a loaf, will give him a stone? Or if he asks for a fish, he will not give him a snake, will he? If you then, being evil, know how to give good gifts to your children,

how much more will your Father who is in heaven give what is good to those who ask him? (Matthew 7:8–11).

James tells us in 4:2b–3, "You do not have, because you do not ask. You ask and do not receive, because you ask with wrong motives, so that you may spend it on your pleasures." We need to examine our heart motive for the things we seek from God. He loves us too much to give us something that will harm our relationship with Him.

How often do we ask God for a need but only after we have squandered His earlier provision for that need? Maybe we were unwise with what we were given by making choices without praying first. Now we are in need because that is the natural consequence of our bad choices. We have acted as unfaithful stewards. Jesus said if we would prove to be good stewards with a little, our Father would entrust us with much (see Luke 16:1–13).

Sometimes we are victims of circumstances beyond our control. As widows, we may find ourselves in a desperate situation as a result of our husband's death. If he was the primary money manager, we may be at the mercy of his management, good or bad. We may find ourselves alone in the clean-up effort, but God's storehouses are full. Let's look at some of the avenues available to us as we try to make sense of our lives from a financial and material perspective.

First we must acknowledge in our heart and mind that everything belongs to God. We must seek His help as we realign our decision-making regarding our finances. We must make our spending decisions a spiritual act.

Principle 5: Get Rid of Debt

Debt is the one area that will probably upset all the others. I will not chastise you about having debt. I had plenty when I started. The first goal, according to the GOIA's fifth principle, is to get rid of debt and stay away from it. With God that is a possible goal. Romans 13:8 says, "Owe nothing to anyone." Proverbs 22:7 tells us that the borrower becomes a servant to the lender, and Jesus said in Matthew 6:24, "No one can serve two masters; for either he will hate the one and love the other, or he will be devoted to one and despise the other. You cannot serve God and wealth."

There are many books available to help you with acquired debt. I have already referred to Larry Burkett's excellent resource, *The Complete Financial Guide for Single Parents*, and I will refer to it later in discussing the unique financial issues facing widows. Mr. Burkett has devoted the second part of this book to the special needs of the widow. Online websites can also be an excellent resource. I recommend **www.crown.org** that offers more personal assistance with financial management. Do the research and find a tool you think will work for you.

Your debt may seem like an impossible task. The key is to be consistent and patient. Make repaying the debt a priority. A pastor once told me that he owed more than $15,000 for a medical debt that was unavoidable. He called his creditor to explain his situation and made a promise to pay a monthly amount within his budget until the debt was paid in full. After several years of faithful payments, the creditor notified him that he had paid sufficiently. Be faithful to what you have promised and leave the rest to the Lord. He is in control, and He knows your situation. He will be faithful to your commitment to honor Him in this matter.

Consolidating your debts into one payment at a low interest rate might be the easiest solution, but it may mean a higher payment than your budget allows. If consolidation will not work for your situation, call your creditors and explain your circumstances. Work with them toward the best interest rate and an agreement to discontinue the addition of late fees added onto the balance. Try to get an affordable adjustment in your monthly payment. I think you'll find that, when given the choice of a high payment that cannot be made or a lower one that gives at least some return, a creditor just wants his money. It is best to pay off the debt with the highest interest rate first. Then as you are able to pay each one off, add that freed-up amount to the next highest bill. Eventually the money you have targeted for debt repayment will accumulate until you finally pay the last bill. Seek God's help. Believe that He can make a difference.

Ideally, though it is not much, you should try to allow five percent of your total net income for debt repayment. Remember, if God truly owns everything, you are actually making your payment to Him. Psalm 50:14–15 says, "Offer to God a sacrifice of thanksgiving; and pay your vows unto the Most High; and call upon Me in the day of trouble; I will rescue you, and you will honor Me."

I made the mistake of trying to make too high a payment on my debt. I wanted to pay it off quickly, but after paying everything extra to it, I didn't have enough money left to make it through the next month. Then I had to go into more debt to get through the month—usually with a VISA card— and my debt just kept building. It was not until I surrendered to a long-term, affordable payment plan that I was finally able to gain success.

Principle 6: Savings and Investments

You should put five percent of your net income into savings. There are three areas you should focus on. First, build a savings account to an amount equal to three months' income. That becomes your emergency fund in case you become ill and cannot work or you lose your job. If you are able to generate any extra income, you can add it to this category. If you become sick or unable to work, you know that you have three months' saved income set aside to pay the bills and some time to put another plan in place. When you go back to work, you need to rebuild the emergency fund.

Once you have accumulated at least three months' income, you should open up a separate savings account for unexpected expenses. The money in this account should be easy to access and have the highest interest rate you can find. You might try setting it up in a money market account that does not require a minimum balance and/or has only a small monthly fee if the balance falls below a required minimum.

The third area of savings/investments is for retirement. If you were already at retirement age when your husband died this is not an issue for you. If you are benefiting from a 401(k) plan, however, you should know that the death of your husband might place you in a higher tax bracket as a single person. Paying out more taxes could then decrease your available income, so be aware of that factor as you plan your budget.

If you are working, take every advantage of building a 401(k) retirement plan through your employer if he provides for it. The maximum amount you can invest is 15 percent of your income up to $11,000 per year. You should be aware that as long as the 401(k) remains with the employer it is safe from personal bankruptcy should that be a threat. Once the 401(k) is rolled over into a tax-deferred IRA at retirement, or when you move to a new place of employment, it will have more flexibility. These plans are very secure. Although you can begin drawing from your 401(k) at 59½, many widows, because of health insurance needs, find it necessary to work until the age of 65 when Medicare is available.

If you have to return to work, another concern may be the care of your children while you are out of the house. As you consider asking family to help, it may be tempting to let grandparents babysit your children. It is very important to realize that children need their grandparents to be just that— grandparents. If you can help it, don't take that relationship from them by putting their grandparents in a role that requires them to be the parent and disciplinarian in your children's lives. They have already lost a father; don't take away the grandparent relationship, too.

When you stay at home, many expenses disappear. Sit down and prayerfully look at all of the figures for both scenarios. Let the Lord lead.

Trust in God

Here is where GOIA principle number six comes into play. As you receive the benefit of your saving and investment choices, do not trust in that inheritance or the people who have been assigned to manage it. Keep your trust in God. He is the one who owns that money. You do not need to worry about how He will manage it. Do not watch it and be obsessed with its activity and the markets that seem to rule it. Even though it may be your source of financial support, God will bless it according to your need and His will for your life. God is in control. Remember that nothing can happen outside of His permission; so trust Him completely.

When my husband was first diagnosed with cancer, we decided that if we were going to trust God completely, we would have to humble ourselves to His ways. No matter what was offered to us, whether money, food, or other resources, we would accept it as from the Lord. Even if we didn't think we needed it, we accepted it. We didn't know what the future would hold and thought God might be giving it to us for the days ahead. We were so blessed by this decision. It was humbling for us, but the protection of that canopy of trust was unbelievable.

For the widow without inheritance the information about Social Security and health insurance is a good start for income options. It is normal to feel timid and unsure if these are uncharted waters for you, but it is very important when dealing with these agencies to demonstrate a sense of confidence. Unfortunately, sometimes you can be denied claims and benefits that are rightfully yours. You must do your homework. Educate yourself on the options you have and trust God to give you the wisdom to do what you need to do.

Principle 7: Giving Is a Gift to the Giver

The Tithe

Perhaps you are unfamiliar with the concept of tithing. The word "tithe" literally means tenth. In the Old Testament one-tenth of everything owned by the nation of Israel was considered holy unto the LORD. At specified times of the year, the nation of Israel was to bring these tithes and offerings to God's "storehouse" for distribution to the Levites and priests, the widows, the fatherless, the orphans, and the poor. This tenth was realized in the form of grain, livestock, and fruits of the harvest as well as money and other assets (see Leviticus 27:27–34, and Malachi 3:10). Giving the tenth was an unquestioned command from God tied to the practices of the Old Testament law.

The word tithe is not mentioned in the New Testament except in reference to this Old Testament command. As the old law and its rigid practices were made complete by Christ's sacrifice on the cross, a new understanding of giving back to the Lord in tithing was also realized. Bringing the tenth, which was holy to the Lord, to the storehouse had now shifted to the heart attitude found in 2 Corinthians 9:7–8, "Each one must do just as he has purposed in his heart, not grudgingly or under compulsion, for God loves a cheerful giver. And God is able to make all grace abound to you, so that always having all sufficiency in everything, you may have an abundance for every good deed." As we can see from this passage, the concept of giving a return did not change, but the way that the return would be managed and who would receive it had dramatically changed.

The amount you choose to give is between you and the Lord. You may choose to use the tenth as a guide. The seventh principle of GOIA is that giving is a gift to the giver. Giving a designated portion off the top tells God you trust Him and are honoring Him by giving back this portion before anything else is spent. The result will be abundance for your own need. Paul tells us that as you supply the needs of the saints, your generosity overflows through many thanksgivings to God (see 2 Corinthians 8:7–15).

Financial Resources

Social Security

Numerous resources are available to widows through Social Security and other health insurance programs provided by federal law. You may not be aware of your rights concerning all these resources. Because the rules for these options are affected by legislative action and frequently change, I will refer you to their websites and you can go online to educate yourself about what they may offer you personally.

Social Security benefits are available to most widows, depending on the specifics of their husband's employment history. The details for eligibility and other information about social security survivor benefits can be found at **www.socialsecurity.gov**.

You may also have help available to you through the Veteran's Administration if your husband qualified. Your husband's base or unit commanders are also compassionate and caring resources for help since they may know you personally. Information on survivor benefits for veterans can be found at **www.military.com**. (Select "benefits" from the home page and go to "survivor benefits.")

Although being a widow is more difficult when there are children in your home, having those children provides a financial advantage through the Social Security resource. Under current regulations, as long as you have a child under 16 you will be given a disbursement for yourself. That is in addition to the benefit that comes to you as guardian for each child who is under 18 or has not yet graduated from high school. There is no longer a benefit for children beyond high school. You will also receive a one-time lump sum death benefit of $225 from Social Security.

At age 60 (50–59 if disabled) you will qualify for a survivor's retirement benefit "based on the person's [your husband's] full Social Security entitlement (full PIA [Primary Insurance Account]), even though [he may have] started receiving benefits before reaching age 65."[2] In addition, if your husband's parents are dependents, they may also qualify for a disbursement.[3] Again, because legislation dictates these benefits, be sure to check with the Social Security Administration for updated information.

You should carefully consider how to manage this money to your full advantage. Having a budget in place with well-defined long-term goals will keep you from squandering your money. Social Security reserves the right to request an accounting of the money at any time, so be a good steward. Create an accounting system that will be easy to track each month. Update your records each time you balance your checkbook while things are still fresh in your mind.

If you have received a significant life insurance payment, try to live on your Social Security disbursements and use the life insurance as a buffer for emergency and investment purposes. If you eliminate your debt, the Social Security benefit may be enough to allow you to remain in your home, raising your children until they graduate from high school.

Be aware that currently, any money you receive and invest in an account for your children as their guardian will have to be liquidated when they reach the age of 18 and returned to Social Security. They will then re-disburse the funds to your children individually. For that reason it might be wiser to save or invest your own personal disbursement as long as you qualify for it and use your children's disbursements for budgeted expenses. This option will obviously be dictated by the age of your youngest child.

Social Security will also provide disbursements for a disabled worker. This disability may be the result of an injury or a terminal disease. Social Security will make monthly payments to you under the following conditions and you should verify these with the Social Security Administration, as the terms may be subject to change.

- The payment will be the same amount you would have been paid had you been retired under normal conditions.
- There are exceptions for persons disabled before reaching age 31 and for the blind.
- At present there is a five-month waiting period, and payments start in the sixth full month of disability. (They are unbending in this requirement.)
- Disability must last (or be expected to last) for at least 12 months or result in death.[4]

If it is at all possible, try to use the Social Security money to stay at home with your children until they lose their disbursement. This is an important time to be there for them. Let God direct you along this course in His wisdom. Maybe His desire is for you to stay at home and generate an additional income from the fruit of your hands. The amount you are able to save may see you through until age 60 when your survivor's retirement investment kicks in.

Health Insurance

Another current source of income for the widow is the health insurance provision required by the COBRA Act, a federal law providing for continuing health insurance coverage. Your husband's employer is required to offer you and your dependents the option of continuing your health insurance through their company at the same rate the company pays. This provision must be extended for eighteen months after the death of your husband. At that time, the company has the option to continue the extension to you, but the rate will be based on individual policy premiums. Many companies provide for this continued extension after the required eighteen months as part of their employee benefit package.

You can get specific details about this law at **www. cobrainsurance.com**. It is worth checking into even if you are limited to only the required eighteen months. You do have to pay the premiums, but it will cost far less than you would have to pay if you purchased an individual health insurance plan. This site also offers options after the COBRA plan expires.

In the past, traditional health insurance outside of an employer has been so expensive that many have had to go without it. If you are trying to be a stay-at-home mom, this might be the obstacle that drives you back to work unless you are willing to look at some less traditional approaches for health insurance.

Here are a few ideas: **www.healthplans.us.com** is a site that offers information on HSAs (health savings accounts) and is a great place for information about these programs and comparative shopping. The development of these accounts is a fairly new concept. HSAs are bank savings accounts that work in tandem with insurance companies to offer insurance with a high deductible that is managed by the tax-deferred savings account. The account is used for health care costs. An employer and employee may pay into this account jointly, or individuals can set up these accounts for themselves.

The advantage of this system is that, because the deductible is so high, the monthly premiums drop dramatically compared to traditional insurance, making it much more affordable. Basically, all of your health costs are paid out of this savings account first. After the deductible is spent, the insurance company you choose pays 100 percent of your health expenses for the remainder of that year, depending on the plan you choose. If you have money in the account at the end of the year, the balance rolls over into the next year, and you can continue to build the high deductible account like you would a regular savings account. The money in the account continues to earn interest and is tax deferred as long as your withdrawal is for health expenses only.

With all these options available to assist you, government funded Medicaid benefits should be used only as a last resort. I believe you should pray a lot before considering this option. Larry Burkett says,

> I personally object to any Christians being forced to take government aid. Although I don't see any specific scriptural prohibition against accepting government aid, I do believe it reflects poorly upon the integrity of the other Christians who have a surplus they could share. As the Apostle Paul said in 2 Corinthians 8:14, "At this present time your abundance being a supply for their want, that their abundance also may become a supply for your want, that there may be equality."[5]

If your church does not have the spiritual maturity to see their responsibility in this light, you need to find a church family that does. Do not let your Christian brethren convince you that you are lazy or at fault in some way for your circumstances. I said in an earlier chapter that God often judged nations or individuals by the way they provided for their widows. It was the fruit of their heart and obedience. Remember that you are a precious widow to your husband, God. He will not forsake you in this hour financially or otherwise.

You may be a widow with an inheritance. If your husband did not plan for how that money was to be invested for your support, the best advice is to put it in time deposits for one year. With your money tied up that first year, you would have time to pray and seek godly counsel about how to manage your money. Once that year has passed, find a wise financial counselor to help you with activating the funds for your benefit.

Budgeting

Once you have identified what your income will be, the next step is to look at budgeting. It is important to approach this area of planning with established biblical principles of money management. To begin, you need to determine your actual gross income on a monthly basis. Gross income is the total money you have to work with every month before taxes or other holdings are taken out. Your net income is the amount you have left after withholdings are deducted. Your tithe to the Lord is determined on your gross income, and your budget will be established from the funds available after withholdings and the tithe.

Having determined what your tithe will be, you can now turn your attention to the process of budgeting. The following budget categories and percentages are taken from Larry Burkett as outlined in his book *The Financial Guide for Single Parents.*[6]

Housing 35%	Savings 5%
Medical/Dental 5%	Miscellaneous 5%
Food 15%	Auto 15%
Health Insurance 5%	Debt 5%
Entertainment 5%	Clothing 5%

Other Expenses

Now you know what your income will be. So with your debt repayment in process and your tithe figure in mind, you can look at your other expenses.

Let's look at housing. The housing allowance should require no more than 35 percent of your net income. This allowance will include utilities, house insurance, home repair, and property taxes. If you think you will need to sell your house, try to hold off for a year before you make a final decision. Be in prayer before the Lord. This is not a time for pride, so let others know about your struggle. God will be faithful and clear about His direction. He comes up with some unbelievable surprises and options.

The food budget should be set at 15 percent of the net income. This may be a good place to cut back if you have to. I include cleaning expenses and personal items in this category. If I can buy it at the grocery store then I include it. Take advantage of the discount stores, cut coupons, and watch for sales. Ask God to help you write out a weekly menu plan and accompanying grocery list. Stick to what is on the list. Pray as you shop. I cannot believe the bargains I find in the store when I ask God to go before me. I ask God to make our food like the loaves and the fishes. When things are short, see if you can get some help from your church food pantry. Making food from scratch is actually more affordable than buying processed and frozen foods. You can make your own TV dinners from leftovers or make them fresh to pull out later and cook. Gardening can also be a cost cutter. Even if you have to plant in containers and set them on the porch or in the yard, it will help on the budget.

Here is another idea. There are a lot of hunters who hunt for the sport and are not necessarily interested in the meat. You may find a deer hunter who would be willing to donate a supply of meat if you pay for the minimal processing costs. You might find a contact by calling a meat processor in the fall during hunting season.

Automobile expenses should consume 15 percent of your net income. This includes car payments, gas, insurance, maintenance, and replacement. You can expect to spend about $600 to $900 on car maintenance every year unless your car is fairly new. Some churches have ministries in place to help singles with minor maintenance needs. If you are making payments on your car you should try to sell it for as much profit as you can. At least try to make enough to pay off the loan. Pray for the Lord to provide a used car you can afford to pay cash for or one that someone may allow you to use until you can afford a dependable used car. Ask your church leaders to help you find a good mechanic who can help you make an informed decision about a used car. Don't discount the salvage yard. Be sure you have someone knowledgeable to determine that the damage to a salvaged car is minimal and will not be a long-term negative factor.

When your car is in need of repair, the rule of thumb is that unless the repair work needed is more than it would cost to replace your car, you should just get it repaired. A used car that is well taken care of should easily get about 200,000 miles of use before you need to think about replacement. This will give you some time to save money for that eventuality. Make sure you change the oil regularly, and when something needs to be fixed, take care of it in a timely manner. Lctting things go with a car can lead to a more costly repair in the long run.

Do your homework on car insurance. You may want to consider liability only on a used car. If your children are going to be driving, they should have a job so they can pay for their own insurance and gas.

Because health insurance is only given five percent of the net income, you may have to make adjustments with some of the other categories. If you are employed, this amount may be enough. If you are not working, perhaps the federal COBRA coverage will be affordable for the required eighteen months until you can research another option.

Medical/Dental is also five percent. This will include expenses insurance does not cover. Talk to your caregivers to make them aware of your concerns. When my daughter had her wisdom teeth out, the bill from the oral surgeon exceeded the insurance allowance. I explained our situation to him and asked whether he was willing to accept the insurance allowance as full payment. He agreed to my request. Our Christian dentist allows us to make extended payments on our dental work. It may be that you can barter for part of your bill. Maybe you can provide babysitting services or office cleaning. Perhaps you can do some filing or other needed office tasks.

Clothing expenses should take another five percent of the net income. This is not much, especially for a family. My husband's grandmother had ten children. She lived in the Appalachian region of West Virginia. She told me one time that every child had three sets of clothing. One they were wearing, one was being washed that day, and one was dirty from the day before. We are very extravagant as a nation when it comes to our clothing. Our closets are full. We often buy designer brands when off-brands will do just as well. There are many good secondhand stores, and most of them are particular about the quality of goods they will accept for sale. Garage sales abound in the summer. Many churches have clothing closets available. Sewing can also be a good way to save. If you don't know how to sew, find someone in your church who can teach you.

Another five percent of your income is allotted to entertainment. I put this amount in an envelope. When the envelope is empty, my expenditure for entertainment is over for the month. Seeing the money helps me spend it more wisely and ration it out over the month.

A provision for miscellaneous items is often overlooked in a budget, yet it cannot be ignored. There is always something needed that doesn't fall into any one category. This allowance should make up five percent of the net income. I try to make a list of miscellaneous items through the month and whittle away at it as the money allows. Some things have to wait until later.

Moving Ahead in Faith

To make these budget ideas work, you must step out in faith. It will not work outside of God's provision. It will stretch you, but it will be exciting to watch the Lord provide. The key is to learn how to wait on Him and His plans for your life. As you learn how to recognize the Lord in the things you once might have called coincidences, your relationship will grow into a deep and trusted dependence. You will become better at reading His signals. Keep His Word close as the standard of measuring every decision.

I think more widows need to share their testimony with other women in the church, explaining what the Lord has taught them. They need to become instruments of warning for those who are unprepared for the same destiny. Be willing to share what you wish you would have known before your husband died. Many couples do not know about the necessity of having a survivorship deed, for example. Many men do not know the best way to title their cars for ownership and how to set up inexpensive life insurance policies so their widows can have an income from the earned interest. Probate issues can be difficult to understand unless preparation has been made ahead of time to avoid them. You may have gained much of this expertise first hand. Let God use you in this area of ministry.

Know that this season of widowhood did not come upon you by accident. God has a purpose in it, and He loves and adores you. I hope that through this book you have learned to receive the words "trust in the Lord" with joy and all sufficiency. I hope you now know how to put feet to your trust. I pray that you will find that this season of widowhood will be one truly set apart by God, a place of privilege in the shelter of the Most High. God Bless!

Study Guide
Chapter 10: Principles of GOIA
(See page vi for instructions for using the study guide.)

1. What Bible truths have you identified as precious promises from Christ for you to believe and act on that relate specifically to the concept of GOIA and your personal finances?

2. Now add the verses you identified from question 1 to your key ring. I hope your key ring verses are well worn from use and will continue to minister to you in the future. By now you may have committed to memory those that have impacted your life in a special way. Continue to use these verses for your personal encouragement and review.

3. Many resources are listed at **www.widowtowidow.net** that you can access at the library or at home. Look in General Financial Resources under the Finance Tab to educate yourself further concerning financial options for income, insurance, and money management. Ask your church leaders to secure for you a reputable financial counselor if that is needed in this process. Be sure to notice the many options and resources Crown Financial Ministries offers at **www.crown.org.**

4. Begin to develop a budget using the following steps:

   • The first step is to go back six months in your checkbook register and credit card statements and create a list of realistic categories for your expenses.

   • Try to identify where each one will fit in the list of categories that I provided for you.

   • Now, using your own real figures, determine what your actual average monthly spending is in each category. This way you will see where you can make realistic adjustments as you begin to apply the percentages. Learn to live within your means and remember that you have a very rich Husband. Don't forget your tithe.

   • Be sure to ask God to direct you in every step and give you the wisdom and discernment you will need to make your budget work. Prayer will be the most important element in this whole exercise and for continuing it in the future. You will need to monitor your budget monthly to make adjustments as you go along.

Additional studies can be accessed at **www. widowtowidow.net** in Chapter Ten under the Study Guide Tab on subjects such as:

- God's Plan for Your Money
- Tithing and New Testament Practices for Money Management
- Budgeting (with access to free budgeting worksheets online).

———————————

Note: another source of encouragement and help can be found at **www.taps.org** (Tragedy Assistance Program for Survivors).

Chapter 11

Conclusion

Summary

❧

W e've covered a lot of ground. Let's recap the main features of this healing process. First and foremost we must identify ourselves on the continuum of victim, survivor, and thriver and do the necessary work to advance to the desired status of emotional and spiritual health. From the position of thriver, we must reexamine our roles and find a footing in our identity in Christ. That will give us a balanced, God-centered perspective. Further, we must get help with any co-dependency that may exist in our relationships with others. Secure in Christ and having taken these major steps, we can confidently proceed to work through our loss with hope.

The ring of verses you collected as we strolled through the Scriptures should already be a daily encouragement to you. Claim those precious promises as you work through your personal struggles. What a hope it is to grasp the full meaning of the truth that God is husband to the widow and father to the fatherless! As women needing affection, conversation, and openness, we now understand that God's marvelous provision is available only as we seek God in a well-developed personal relationship. And only with this close relationship will we be able to fight the daily spiritual battles with fear, worry, discouragement, anxiety, anger, and depression.

By now, the practical implications of trusting God should have become realities. When they do, the issues that drive us toward idolatry seem to take care of themselves. We realize that God has great resources for our eternal welfare. We are now living in the full knowledge of His sufficient provision. With this God-centered life we can begin to make sense of our suffering and loss.

Embracing the Desolate Place

In the Hebrew text, the word for widow is *"almânâh"* (al-maw-naw´). According to Strong's Concordance, it means a desolate place, a desolate house.[1] It is an apt description of the season of widowhood we have entered. The word "desolate" itself conjures pictures of wastelands without life or hopeless places of sorrow and abandonment. If we are honest, don't we sometimes feel like that describes us? In contrast to our desire to escape this desolate place of widowhood, Scripture reveals that Jesus seemed to welcome the desolate places He encountered. He emerged from them with renewed power, direction, and strength.

Throughout His ministry Jesus slipped away from His disciples and the crowds. Often He retreated to be alone in a quiet place, a mountain, a desert, or another desolate place. These desolate places were actually havens of refuge where He regained strength. God was there, waiting to strengthen and give direction.

In Matthew chapter four, Jesus is in the wilderness being tempted. Though this was a place of darkness and evil, He went willingly. It is comforting to know that Jesus was not alone, for the Spirit of God led him to this place. God charged the angels to obey the command of Christ at any moment. After the temptation, the angels ministered to Jesus, and He emerged from His wilderness experience eager to begin His Kingdom work. We should be comforted to know that God compassionately dispatches those same ministering servants on our behalf as He oversees the days of our widowhood.

On one occasion, Jesus withdrew from His disciples to a lonely place by Himself. The multitudes, seeking compassion and healing, found Him. The disciples were aware that there was no food in this desolate place, and they pleaded with Jesus to send the multitudes away. Instead, He performed one of His greatest miracles, feeding the multitude of more than 5,000 people with only five loaves of bread and two fish. Exhausted by the crowds with their demands, He sent the disciples ahead of Him across the sea. Again, he retreated to the mountain by Himself to pray. Scripture says, "When it was evening, He was there alone" (Matthew 14:23).

Jesus' ministry was continually empowered by the time He spent alone in the desolate places. It was there He entered the presence of God. In the same manner, we must embrace the desolate place of our widowhood. It is the place of God's presence, renewal, and preparation for the months and years to come. We don't know the plan, but we know the Master. He is our Redeemer; He is our Husband. "His compassions never fail. They are new every morning" (Lamentations 3:22–23). May you meet His powerful presence in your desolate place.

Endnotes

Chapter 1

[1] From author's notes from Gregory Schad workshop, "Care When It's Critical: Helping Others Recover from Trauma" (Columbus, Ohio: Citywide Training Facility), July 10-11, 2002.

[2] Elizabeth-Kubler Ross, *On Death and Dying* (New York: Touchstone, 1969).

[3] Gregory Schad, workshop notebook, p. 16.

[4] Ibid., workbook p. 16.

[5] Ibid., workbook p. 16.

[6] Ibid., workbook p. 16.

[7] Author's notes from workshop

[8] James Strong, *Strong's Exhaustive Concordance* (Grand Rapids: Baker Book House, 1992), Greek dictionary reference number 4100, p. 58.

[9] Taken from *Boundaries* by John Townsend; Henry Cloud. Copyright © 1992 by Henry Cloud and John Townsend, Used by permission of The Zondervan Corporation.

[10] Ibid.

Chapter 2

[1] James Strong, *Strong's Exhaustive Concordance* (Grand Rapids: Baker Book House, 1992), Greek dictionary reference number 3340/3341, p. 47.

[2] Hannah Whitall Smith, *The Christian's Secret of a Happy Life.* (Urichsville, Ohio: Barbour Publishing, Inc.), p. 81.

Chapter 3

[1] *All the Women of the Bible:* Taken from *All the Women of the Bible* by Herbert Lockyer . Copyright © Printed 97 98 99 00 01 02/DH/54 53 52. Used by permission of Zondervan. p. 47.

[2] James Strong, *Strong's Exhaustive Concordance* (Grand Rapids: Baker Book House, 1992), Greek dictionary reference numbers 5490/5503, p. 77.

[3] Ibid., Greek dictionary reference number 3689, p. 52.

[4] Stanley Cornils, "Does Your Church Take Care of its Widows?" *Christianity Today*, July 15, 1983, p. 60.

Chapter 5

[1] Neil T. Anderson, and Dave Park, *Stomping out the Darkness* (Ventura, Calif.: Gospel Light/Regal Books, 1993), p. 113, Used by permission.

[2] Ibid., p. 113.

[3] Ibid., pp. 113-114.

[4] Ibid., p. 114.

[5] Ibid., p. 118.

[6] By permission. From Merriam-Webster's Collegiate® Dictionary, 10th Edition ©2002 by Merriam-Webster, Incorporated.

[7] Smith, p. 115.

[8] Hannah Whitall Smith, *The Christian's Secret of a Happy Life* (Urichsville, Ohio: Barbour Publishing, Inc., 1875), p. 35-36.

[9] Ibid., pp. 37-38.

[10] Ibid., chapter 7, *passim*

Chapter 6

[1] Hannah Whitall Smith. *The Christian's Secret to a Happy Life* (Urichsville, Ohio: Barbour Publishing, 1875), p. 141.

[2] Ibid., p. 137.

[3] Ibid., p. 138.

[4] Ibid., p. 140.

Chapter 7

[1] Harley, p. 30.

[2] Willard F. Harley, Jr., *His Needs, Her Needs; Building An Affair-Proof Marriage* (Grand Rapids: Baker Book House, 2000 edition by Revell), p.13

[3] Taken from *Life Lessons on the Life and Ministry of the Messiah* (video series) by Ray Vander Laan. Copyright © 1996 by Ray Vander Laan. Used by permission of Zondervan.

[4] Vander Laan, from Vol. 3.

[5] U.S. Census Bureau, *Statistical Abstract of the United States*: 121st Edition; November 2001, table No. 49 ("Marital Status of the Population by Sex, Race, and Hispanic Origin": 1980 to 2000), p. 47

[6] Larry Burkett, *The Complete Financial Guide for Single Parents* (Wheaton: Victor Books, 1992), p. 150.

[7] Ibid., p. 130.

Chapter 8

[1.] Personal Internet communication entitled *Push,* April 4, 2001.
[2] Hannah Whitall Smith, *The Christian's Secret of a Happy Life.* (Urichsville, Ohio: Barbour Publishing, 1875), p. 118.

Chapter 9

[1] James Strong, *Strong's Exhaustive Concordance* (Grand Rapids: Baker Book House, 1992), Greek dictionary reference number 4390, p. 66.

Chapter 10

[1] Pastor Mike Gauch, Sermon on Financial Management, January 2002, *passim.*
[2] Larry Burkett, *The Complete Financial Guide for Single Parents* (Wheaton, Ill: Victor Books, 1992), p. 189.
[3] Ibid., p. 189
[4] Ibid., p. 189
[5] Ibid., p. 110
[6] Ibid. pp. 108-118, *passim.*

Chapter 11

[1] James Strong, *A Concise Dictionary of the Hebrew Bible* in *Strong's Exhaustive Concordance* (Grand Rapids: Baker Book House, 1992), reference number 490, p. 13.

www.widowtowidow.net

- ᔣ **Newsletter**—Articles and Testimonials
- ᔣ **Bible Studies**—Engaging Widows' Issues
- ᔣ **Interactive Posting**—Widow to Widow
- ᔣ **Pastor Resources**—Ministry that Impacts Widows
- ᔣ **Website Resources**—Empowered to Act

Email Us At:

almanaheart@widowtowidow.net

Share how you actively minister to the widows in your church and community. If you are a widow we are interested in knowing about your circumstances so we can encourage and support you.

This website has been designed as a tool for widows who are working through loss as well as for the families, friends, and pastors who desire to encourage and support them. *Widow-to-Widow Ministries* desires to be a facilitator in connecting the pastors and widows of today's church culture according to the model outlined in Acts 6 and James 1:27.